Developing Emotional Intelligence

Developing Emotional Intelligence

How to Retrain Your Brain to Win Friends, Influence People, Improve your Social Skills, Achieve Happier Relationships, and Raise Emotionally Intelligent Children

Mark T. Coleman PhD

Mark T. Coleman PhD

CONTENTS

ONE

Practical Guide to improve Emotional Intelligence

1. Introduction — 5
2. Emotional Intelligence Essential Facts — 7
3. Emotional Intelligence — 19
4. The Emotional Intelligence Framework — 31
5. What is an Emotional Intelligence Test? — 43
6. Measuring Emotional Intelligence — 53
7. Emotional Intelligence Self-Assessment — 63
8. 50 Practical Tips to Improve Self-Awareness — 75
9. 50 Practical Tips to Improve Self-Management — 85
10. 50 Practical Tips to Improve Social Awareness — 95

CONTENTS

11 | 50 Practical Tips to Improve Relationship Management 105

12 | Conclusion 113

TWO

Emotional Intelligence for Kids

13 | Introduction 117

14 | How is emotional intelligence developed 121

15 | Raising emotionally intelligent children 131

16 | Parenting styles in regards to Emotional Intelligence 143

17 | Marriage, Divorce and your Child's Emotional health 151

18 | The Father's crucial role 159

19 | Assessing the Effectiveness of Your Parenting Style 167

20 | Emotion Coaching Elements 179

21 | Emotion Coaching Strategies 189

22 | Emotion Coaching as Your Child Grows 199

CONTENTS

23 Recommended Children's Books to Help with Emotional Intelligence and Emotion Coaching 213

24 Conclusion 217

© Copyright 2021 by Mark T. Coleman PhD - All rights reserved.

The following Book is reproduced below with the goal of providing information that is as accurate and reliable as possible. Regardless, purchasing this Book can be seen as consent to the fact that both the publisher and the author of this book are in no way experts on the topics discussed within and that any recommendations or suggestions that are made herein are for entertainment purposes only. Professionals should be consulted as needed prior to undertaking any of the action endorsed herein.

This declaration is deemed fair and valid by both the American Bar Association and the Committee of Publishers Association and is legally binding throughout the United States.

Furthermore, the transmission, duplication, or reproduction of any of the following work including specific information will be considered an illegal act irrespective of if it is done electronically or in print. This extends to creating a secondary or tertiary copy of the work or a recorded copy and is only allowed with the express written consent from the Publisher. All additional right reserved.

The information in the following pages is broadly considered a truthful and accurate account of facts and as such, any inattention, use, or misuse of the information in question by the reader will render any resulting actions solely under their purview. There are no scenarios in which the publisher or the original author of this work can be in any fashion deemed liable for any hardship or damages that may befall them after undertaking information described herein.

Additionally, the information in the following pages is intended only for informational purposes and should thus be thought of as universal. As befitting its nature, it is presented without assurance regarding its prolonged validity or interim quality. Trademarks that are mentioned are done without written consent and can in no way be considered an endorsement from the trademark holder.

ONE

Practical Guide to improve Emotional Intelligence

1

Introduction

Have you ever had a time where you reacted poorly in an emotionally charged situation, and your reaction resulted in a situation that you wish was different? Perhaps you have had a bad day at work, and when you got home, you lashed out at your spouse and children out of frustration when they played a game just a bit too loudly for your taste.

Though they were having a blast playing together, they annoyed you, and you said things you regret. As a result, your children went to bed upset with you after calling you a meanie-head and saying they wished you were still at work, and you angered your spouse, who chose to sleep on the couch instead of in bed with you. After your outburst, you are left with the guilt weighing on your conscience, a wish to change on your mind, and the assumption that the kind of change you would like to see is an impossibility in your heart. You may feel as though you are not the person your family deserves due to your inability to deal with emotional situations.

The reason you reacted so poorly to the situation is due to a low level of emotional intelligence. Emotional intelligence is believed to be one of the most accurate predictors of success and happiness in life, and those who are lacking average or high levels of emotional intelligence often find themselves struggling socially, especially when emotions are running high. We all have natural levels of emotional intelligence, influenced by upbringing and general temperament, much like how we have natural levels of intelligence, but unlike intelligence, emotional intelligence levels are flexible.

You can build your emotional intelligence and influence your ability to read and react to emotional situations. This means that you can improve your EQ (emotional quotient; the measurement of your emotional intelligence), and improve your social skills and relationships, though it will take effort.

Imagine if you had a higher EQ in the above situation: You would have come home from work angry, but instead of lashing out at your family, you took a deep breath, recognized that your family was having fun, and went to take a quiet drive around town for fifteen minutes to yourself to unwind before returning home and joining in on playtime and your children's bedtime routines. Instead of them being upset and angry at you, your children told you they love you, told you that you are the best, and went to bed happily. You then were able to spend time with your spouse, calmly explaining the situation and why you were angry, which gained you the emotional support of your spouse as well. Ultimately, you were able to handle the situation tactfully, and despite the anger you felt, you bettered your relationships with your spouse and children.

With the help of this part, you will be provided the skills you will need to bolster your EQ and develop the ability to handle social situations with tact. You will be guided through the basics of EQ, provided tests to see where your current EQ levels are, and then given plenty of tips to improve on your EQ levels. You are not destined to remain at low levels of EQ forever; putting in the effort to boost your skills is entirely possible, and you can achieve the high EQ you and those around you deserve.

2

Emotional Intelligence Essential Facts

Before delving into what emotional intelligence is and how it works, you must first learn to understand the concepts that underlie it. Every person feels emotions and has a unique temperament, and most people experience empathy in some capacity. These combine and create your reactions to emotionally volatile situations. Each of these relates intricately with emotional intelligence and having an understanding of what causes these and why we have them is a key to raising it. By knowing how these relate to emotional intelligence, you can work with them as opposed to against them, seeing much quicker progress than going in blindly. Those with low EQ are typically slaves to their temperaments and emotions and react as such, whereas those who have a high EQ are typically much more empathetic and in control over both themselves and their situations.

Understanding Emotions

There are several human emotions, all composed of basic emotions that can combine into a wide spectrum of what is felt from day to day. It is believed that emotions can be reduced down to four basic feelings: happiness, sadness, anger, and fear. Every emotion you may feel, from surprise to guilt or disgust, are all subsets of those four emotions. These four are believed to be biologically ingrained into us through evolution, though it is possible to develop more nuanced or complicated feelings through sociological sources, such as cultural influence.

The Purpose of Emotions

These four emotions must be important if they have evolved over time to be universal: Almost any human from any culture can see a picture of another human making any of those four expressions and know exactly what it is. The reason for this is to be able to quickly and clearly communicate with other humans. By developing both expressions of universal emotions, humans pave the way to develop empathy as well.

Each of the four universal emotions conveys something different: They identify different situations and needs. Happiness conveys that all needs are being met. Sadness conveys that something bad has happened or something or someone important has been lost or harmed and indicates that there is a need for support to encourage healing. Anger conveys the sense of being wronged, whether being taken advantage of or getting betrayed, and it indicates a need for boundaries or protection. Fear conveys that there is a threat or danger nearby and that there is a need for safety.

As a social species, we need to be able to communicate our basic needs in order to ensure everyone's needs are met. If we do not know how our neighbors are doing, we never know whether they need extra help or support, or if we are angering them and need to take a step back. Through communication, everyone's needs are met more efficiently, and the easiest way to communicate those needs is through universal body language. With body language and emotions, we can see, at a glance, how those around us are feeling. We can also tell the intentions of strangers by being able to see signs of anger on their expressions, or if they are happy, scared, or sad. Communicating at a glance without needing to observe and process words or more convoluted forms of communication allows for quick snap-judgments to be made, enabling for quicker reactions as well.

Emotions also have internal connotations as well. These can encourage or motivate us to act in certain ways, as well as help general survival. If you feel afraid, your body prepares to flee or fight in order to keep you alive. If you are angry, your body prepares to protect itself. Happiness causes relaxation and encourages you to engage in more of the behaviors that triggered the happiness, to begin with, and sadness encourages us to protect those we love or change our situations to something that brings us joy.

The Cause of Emotions
There are several different theories on what causes emotions, but the three most common are the James-Lange theory, the Cannon-Bard theory, and the Schacter-Singer model. Each of these is slightly different and offer various explanations.

The James-Lange Theory believes that emotion is a person's understanding of the physiological changes the body creates in response to a stimulus. If a person sees a snake and feels his extremities begin to tingle, his heart race, and his breathing quicken as he hyper-focuses on the snake in front of him, he knows that what he is physically feeling is fear and responds in that manner. In this theory, the physical changes come first, and the mind labels the physical changes as the emotion in order to understand them.

The Cannon-Bard theory believes that we sense things around us with our five senses, and the information sensed is sent through the nervous system to the brain, where two different parts receive the message. The cortex, or the front of the brain, receives one message and responds to the message while the hypothalamus receives a second copy of the message and creates the physical reactions. In this case, the man sees the snake. His eyes send the message that he has seen a snake to both his cortex and hypothalamus.

The cortex creates the emotion in response to the stimulus while the hypothalamus creates the physical response. The physical and emotional responses combine together to create the emotion of fear.

The Schacter-Singer model believes that fear is a combination of physical responses to a stimulus paired with conscious thoughts on the stimulus. The two of these together create a general feeling toward the stimulus, which is interpreted as the emotion. For example, the man who has seen a snake may feel his heartbeat quicken in response to the snake, but his feeling depends on his cognitive thoughts on the idea of snakes. If he believes that snakes are quite fascinating and loves to look at them, that heartbeat quickening may be interpreted as happiness, but if he has learned that snakes are dangerous and should be avoided at all costs, that same increase in pulse combined with those beliefs would create a feeling of fear.

James-Lange Theory	Emotion is the person's interpretation of physical changes to the body in response to a stimulus
Cannon-Bard Theory	The body sends information from the senses to the cortex, which creates emotion, and hypothalamus of the brain, which creates physical responses such as crying or shaking in fear
Schacter-Singer Model	Emotion is created when physical changes and conscious thoughts over a stimulus combine

Conflict of Rationality vs. Emotionality

Oftentimes, in our minds, we are constantly hovering somewhere between rational and emotional. The emotional part of our minds was born first, designed to keep us alive long enough to reproduce. The rational part of our minds is what makes us distinctly human: It allows us the ability to act in ways that are contradictory to our emotions in order to get a better result. We allow emotions to influence our thoughts and decisions, but allow the rational part of our minds to police the emotional part to keep it in balance. In order to be successful people, especially in workplaces and relationships, we need a healthy balance between both rationality and emotionality. Sometimes, however, we find our sense of rationality drowned out by the emotional side of our minds. In this instance, the person would be entirely enslaved to the emotions. Consider that the person afraid of snakes has a snake phobia, and upon seeing a harmless garden snake slither in front of him, goes into a panic attack and freezes at the sight. In this case, he was ruled by his emotions; his rational side of his brain, which would have reminded him that the snake is tiny and harmless, was silenced by the emotion of fear.

The Relevance of Emotions to Emotional Intelligence

This battle of rationality and emotionality relates directly to emotional intelligence: It is the ability to identify those emotions, manage them, and balance them in such a way that allows for rational thinking. A high EQ means that you are likely to be adept at managing your emotions and giving them the consideration they deserve while still keeping them in check and allowing rationality to rule. This allows for level-headedness, which allows the man afraid of snakes to simply walk away mildly perturbed at having seen a snake, but still fully capable of functioning.

Understanding Empathy

Empathy is the ability to understand and feel another person's feelings as if you, yourself, were experiencing them. Empathy allows you to take one look at a grieving widow and feel her pain strongly enough to motivate you to help her, or that allows you to feel proud and happy for your child who made it onto the varsity basketball team when he comes to tell you the good news, his own face alight with unadulterated joy.

There are five key components of empathy: Understanding others, developing others, service orientation, leveraging diversity, and political awareness. These together combine to create the empathy that you feel for others. It is a skill that can be developed, though it should come naturally to some degree.

The Purpose of Empathy
Empathy exists to keep us cognizant of others' needs. We use empathy to allow us to look at a person near us and understand how they are feeling, which in turn, cues us in on what that person may be needed at that particular moment. By understanding how someone is feeling through empathy, we are able to relate to other people within our social groups, and that motivates us to help them meet their own needs. It instills this sense of compassion within us that encourages us to tend to others and behave selflessly. This selflessness enables larger groups of people to survive. It is that inherent desire to ensure that your partners, friends, children, and other loved ones are cared for, which helps further ensure their own survival.

Empathy goes a step further in ensuring survival as well: It allows for labor to be tailored to individuals' strengths, fully expecting each to contribute to the society's survival in a meaningful fashion. Instead of each person having to go out and survive on his or her own without help, empathy, and society allows for each person to specialize. One person may hunt while another focuses on farming and yet another works on general construction and maintenance of the village. Someone else entirely may make the food that the hunter and farmer provide, and ultimately, everyone ends up with a variety of needs met while only having to specialize in one task. From an evolutionary standpoint, empathy is one of the main reasons humanity has developed as far as it has: People no longer have to do everything in order to survive and can instead specialize.

The doctor does not have to worry about hunting to make sure he has food so he can focus on medical care. The hunter does not have to worry about making clothing so she can focus solely on providing food. The teacher does not have to worry about food or shelter and can instead tend to children. In today's society, it takes a village to meet all needs, and empathy is what enables us to do so.

Empathy and Emotional Intelligence

Empathy is one of the key components of emotional intelligence. Empathy acts as the bond between yourself and those around you, and that ability to understand those around you as though you yourself were in his or her shoes. This enables you to deepen your bonds with other people, which can be the key to building a higher EQ. Consider the man who came home from work angry that was discussed in the introduction: Had he stopped and considered how the person with whom he had fought at work had felt, he may have been able to respond better. If the two of them fought over part of their work not being done because each believed the other would take care of it, the man could have stopped to consider that maybe his coworker had been confused and it was all a big misunderstanding. Through empathy, you are able to better control your own emotions because you are aware of how they impact those around you. You can see and feel the hurt you inflict when you act impulsively or out of anger or fear. Likewise, you feel good when those around you feel good, making you more interested in meeting the needs of others.

Understanding Temperament

Temperament describes an individual's nature: It is how he or she behaves naturally. It is primarily inherited genetically, creating traits that were either nurtured or developed early in life, or that came innately. Temperament is particularly tricky as it is a predisposition for a specific type of behavior, though it does not necessarily guarantee that whatever you are predisposed toward is going to happen. Here are four examples of temperament in action:

The Purpose of Temperament

Temperament provides your base personality. It is your inherent preferences and dislikes, how you react to crowds, whether you enjoy sports, how you react to certain stimuli, and so much more. Your temperament is essentially your basic foundation for your personality. You can be introverted or extroverted, athletic, stubborn, easygoing, submissive, or so many more different traits. The temperament serves that basis and dictates our reactions. Someone who is shy is not likely to enjoy herself at a school dance and will probably do anything possible to skip or leave early, whereas someone who is hardheaded and dominant is likely going to thrive in some sort of leadership position, and will actively avoid any situations that would require submission. Your temperament cues other people to respond to you in certain ways, while you likely take the same cues from other people's temperaments. The important part to remember is that while you can shape your own temperament, you cannot outright change it. While your temperament does influence your behavior, what it does is determine how you do something rather than what you choose to do. Your temperament is not an excuse for poor behavior, but it will provide you with insight to understand why you have the tendencies you do.

The Cause of Temperament

Temperament is believed to be largely inherited, but also is related to the environment in which you may find yourself and also life experience, particularly in the younger years. Together, genetics or biological predispositions, physical attributes, environment, and early life experiences come together to form your temperament. Someone with a biological predisposition toward caution or anxiety who is born into a stressful environment and spent much of early childhood crying as parents argued is likely to grow into an anxious person, whereas that same child could have been generally happy but somewhat cautious or slow to warm up to situations had the parents been less combative and the home more relaxed and encouraging in the early years. Overall, the four traits combine and create a person's base personality or temperament.

The Relevance of Temperament to Emotional Intelligence

Those who have a lower EQ are typically enslaved to their temperament. Their EQ may not be enough to mitigate damaging or destructive behaviors, and they react emotionally instead of rationally. They will almost always behave in ways that come naturally thanks to their temperament. This is not always a good thing: The shy person becomes unable to overcome her fear of social events and may struggle in formal professional or academic settings.

The hardheaded person may ruin relationships due to being entirely unwilling to compromise or admit when he is wrong. These can lead to catastrophic results in which the people are unsuccessful and unhappy with their lives, and the people around them are equally as unhappy.

On the other hand, people with higher levels of emotional intelligence are able to more or less override their base temperaments. While they, as a whole, are still shy or hardheaded, they are able to work past those temperaments to do what they need to do.

The shy person may be a fantastic HR director, despite hating social interaction, because she is able to look past that anxiety she feels when confronted with people or problems and instead, with empathy and compassion, decides to help other people rather than cave to her own introverted nature. The hardheaded man may hate conceding, but be willing to do so when he can rationalize that he is, in fact, wrong. By having higher levels of emotional intelligence, people are able to acknowledge their feelings and their temperaments for what they are, but they are able to use the rational part of their minds to overcome them when necessary or when it is beneficial to do so.

3

Emotional Intelligence

We are all born with an inherent understanding of basic emotions. Even deaf and blind babies who may never have been exposed to sound or seeing a smile naturally show emotions the same way as grown adults: They cry when they need something or are afraid and smile at things that make them happy. This capacity for understanding and expressing emotions is hardwired into them in order to help them survive, and that understanding is used constantly.

You naturally seek to read other people's emotions in every interaction you have. Have you ever approached someone who appeared to be in a foul mood and felt that moment of apprehension toward interacting with him or her? Or have you ever seen someone so happy that you could not help but smile and feel a little more at ease? Your mind unconsciously reads the body language of everyone around you, responding to the tiniest differences in expressions and the positions of the body, whether someone is tense with their head up or down, where the hands are, and so on. That instant understanding at a glance comes from emotional intelligence. It helps us navigate society without stepping on other people's emotional toes left and right, and helps enable us to live as a successful society and ensure that everyone's needs are met.

Defining Emotional Intelligence

Simply put, emotional intelligence is the ability to regulate the emotions of yourself and others, being able to accurately define other people's emotions, and using emotional feedback to influence your own thoughts and behaviors, as well as the behaviors of others. You are able to recognize your own emotional states and use that feedback to guide your reactions in order to make the best possible decisions on what kinds of behaviors you should exhibit. You are able to control your own emotions and utilize them to ensure that your own needs are met. It also allows you to handle your relationships with other people with tact, which betters interpersonal relationships.

Further simplified, emotional intelligence is being aware of the fact that emotions have a massive amount influence on everything you do. Your own thoughts and behaviors are heavily influenced by your emotions and recognizing that while being able to keep your own emotions in check enables you to behave in ways that are conducive to fixing problems that may be influencing your emotions in a negative manner.

Emotional intelligence, when all aspects are combined, create leaders. People with high EQs in each of the main constructs of emotional intelligence are typically much better at leadership roles than those with lower EQs. Each of the constructs combine to create a well-rounded individual that is concerned with the welfare of those around him or her, able to balance the needs of those around him or her, and able to manage everyone and motivate them to act in ways that are conducive to the group's success as a whole.

Importance of Emotional Intelligence

You may be asking yourself why emotional intelligence matters. If you are able to innately understand basic emotions and those emotions have very specific purposes, why does it matter whether you can influence them? If they are evolutionarily important, why override them? Would that not be counterproductive to our very nature as human beings? Yes and no; emotions are important and should be given consideration as they often have very important implications, but at the same time, if all we do is give in to our emotions, which are, all things considered, quite fickle, we become impulsive and unproductive. Relationships suffer when we respond to people because we were momentarily angry at them. We say things in anger that we may not mean. Sadness and grief can be completely crippling if we act upon them. Happiness and enjoyment can lead to destructive behaviors such as drug abuse, but can also destroy careers if all you ever do is what makes you happy with no regard to responsibilities. Fear can render you paralyzed when what you need to do is act in order to save yourself or others you care about.

These emotions are important biologically, but humans have developed to the point that we can think critically and rationally. If we only reacted based on emotions, we would be crippling our own potential. Think of how a toddler behaves: He is likely impulsive and gives in to every feeling that passes, as that is all he knows. He does not know how to control his emotions, and his need for instant gratification leads to all sorts of trouble. Toddlers may hit, scream, throw temper tantrums, steal, or put themselves in danger impulsively. They do not have that capacity for rational thought that humans develop throughout early adulthood. Denying that rationality and refusing to act upon it is to deny humanity itself. You have developed the ability to understand the relationships between how you feel, your general temperament, the situation at hand, and your behaviors, and you are able to influence that with rational thought.

Being able to influence all of your behaviors with rational thought means you are not a slave to instinct. You can act selflessly to aid someone else, though your instincts are screaming at you to leave. You can be a leader that recognizes the feelings of everyone around you and leads with compassion and empathy rather than through dominance. Your behaviors are the keys to all interpersonal relationships, and when you can control those behaviors with high EQ, you can better influence your relationships and be more successful in social situations. High EQ allows you to be more efficient at resolving conflicts, and empathize better with others. By having better relationships with those around you, you are more likely to be happy and relaxed. You are more likely to be healthier, both physically and mentally, because you are happier in your relationships and more secure in your place in society.

Ultimately, there is not a single aspect of your life that is not touched in some way by emotional intelligence. It impacts everything, whether you are conscious of it or not. EQ influences your success both socially and professionally; sometimes more than IQ does, and understanding its importance is critical to understanding why developing a higher EQ is so crucial to being successful in life.

Applications of Emotional Intelligence

Understanding how EQ can impact various aspects of relationships is crucial to seeing just how profoundly it can impact your life. This section will provide what high EQ looks like in each of the following situations and contrast it with what may happen when someone with lower EQ is also in the same situation. The difference between the two can be staggering when compared side-by-side.

EQ in Romantic Relationships

Imagine you and your spouse are arguing again. Your spouse is a stay at home parent to young children while you work full time during standard office hours. Each day, you come home, and your spouse asks for help as soon as you walk in the door. You can see that your spouse looks stressed, still wearing dirty pajamas, dinner is on the stove, cooking, and the living room looks like a bomb exploded with toys. The children are bickering, and your spouse quickly shoves the children at you and hands you the spatula before disappearing to the bathroom, shutting and locking the door and turning on the shower.

Assuming you have a lower EQ, you may immediately get angry. After all, you have just come home from work, and you are mentally drained from a day of office work. Your spouse got to stay home, you tell yourself angrily, and it looks as though your spouse has gotten nothing done all day. The home is trashed, the children are not fed, and dinner is not finished. In your anger, you follow your spouse to the bathroom and proceed to yell through the door. You do not recognize that your spouse had looked stressed prior to leaving or consider that all that your spouse had heard all day was the sound of the very children bickering that was skyrocketing your own anger. The children hear you screaming through the door and run away to cry. Your spouse does not open the door. Dinner burns on the stove. All of that compounds on your anger and makes it worse. Your relationships with both your spouse and your children have been harmed. Your spouse feels as though you are not supportive, and your children learn to avoid you because you are an angry person.

Stop and think about how the situation would have played out had you had a higher EQ. You would have walked through the door and seen the desperation painted across your spouse's face. You would have been able to feel the stress, and anxiety practically emanating from your spouse and see how overwhelmed your spouse was with the situation. Instead of getting angry, you would have seen that what your spouse needed was a quick reprieve from the constant nagging of children. You would have happily entertained the children, and the change in pace may have been enough to stop their bickering. You would have finished up dinner, getting it plated and serving the children, who happily ran to eat. Your spouse would have emerged from the shower feeling much more at ease and ready to tackle the rest of the evening, and would have felt supported and loved because you had taken the initiative to alleviate some of the stress. Your relationship, instead of being hurt, was strengthened by your ability to deescalate the situation. Furthermore, your children learn that marriage is a partnership. The tit-for-tat sort of comparison is harmful, and what a marriage needs is for both partners to look out for each other's needs, even when they are not verbally expressed, and even when they may not be convenient.

EQ in Familial Relationships

Imagine that your children have been misbehaving all day. They keep running through the house, as children do when they are cooped up indoors due to bad weather, and no matter how often you tell them to stop, you can hear the thudding of their quick footsteps running down the hallway again minutes later. After the umpteenth time of reminding them to stop and enjoying the momentary reprieve from the constant thumps of their feet, you hear their running start again, followed by a loud bang, and glass shattering. You rush out and see that your children because they were not listening, ran into the hutch and knocked out an entire row of wine glasses, which shattered all over the floor.

Assuming you have low EQ, you are likely to run out and yell. Immediately you scream at the children for not listening, chewing them out for their disobedience ruining everything and telling them to look at the mess they left for you. Despite the fear, pain, and guilt on their faces, you belittle them for not listening, say something along the lines of accusing them of not being good kids or wishing they were not there, and you yell at them both to go to their rooms for the rest of the night. Your children stare at you in horror for a moment before breaking down into tears and running away. You ignored the fact that one of the children had a cut on her foot and the other was terrified of you, and you ignored the damage that your outburst had to your children. As your children aged, they sought to put more and more distance between you and them, until they eventually left and cut off contact due to your abusive tendencies during their childhood.

With higher EQ, you would have ran out to see what happened, and immediately ask if your children are okay. You would have surveyed them, picked each up out of the glass, and taken them to the other room to patch them up while having a serious, but still calm, conversation about this being the reason you asked them not to play so roughly indoors. Instead of losing your temper, you used the incident to teach the children a lesson. When they were all patched up, you took them back to the mess and asked them to help you clean it up in an age-appropriate manner. Each child contributed to the mess, and they each sincerely apologized. You gave your children hugs, reminded them that you love them, and told them sternly to avoid running indoors. They nodded and left to go play by themselves, feeling secure in their attachment to you, and having learned a very valuable lesson. You strengthened your relationship with your children, and they have learned that they can rely on you in moments of need thanks to your level-headed response to what was a messy situation.

EQ in Platonic Relationships

Imagine that you are setting up for your friend to come over to your house for an evening of video games, a few beers, and some pizza. It is a very low-key event meant to be relaxing. The time that your friend was supposed to arrive came and went, and almost an hour later, he finally shows up. He looks upset about something and mutters an apology, but entirely avoids the topic of why he was late. Instead, he grabs a beer, sits down silently to watch you play the game. He downs the beer and then grabs another without a word. He glances at his phone off and on, his expression darkening every time he does.

If you have a lower EQ, you may respond to this negatively. You are hurt that your friend was late and offered no apology or explanation. You are angry that you feel devalued. You are sad that your friend seems to not care that you are feeling upset about his actions. Instead of looking at him and seeing his own feelings, you look at him and snap. You tell him that if he doesn't want to be there, and it looks like that is the case, then he can just leave because you do not need his negativity bringing down the mood when you wanted to have a good time. You tell him off for checking his phone so often and tell him that he is an awful friend and that you refuse to put up with such disrespect. In response, your friend does not say a word. He picks up his phone, looks as though he might cry, and walks out. He never texts you again, never answers when you call and refuses to acknowledge you every time you ever see him out and about. He ended the friendship over your outburst.

With a higher EQ, you may have looked at the situation and seen that your friend was not doing well. At a glance, you would have been able to see the hurt in his expression upon walking through your door, and you would have been more willing to provide him with the support he must have needed. Despite the annoyance you felt, you also understood that your friend was not doing well, and that superseded your annoyance. Even if he did not want to talk about what had happened, you would have seen that what he really needed in that moment was to be supp0rted during some sort of personal struggle. Instead of putting him down, you would have patiently waited for him to share whatever had happened, and while you waited, you would have continued gaming and genuinely enjoying your friend's company. Eventually, he would eventually open up about having a fight with his fiancée prior to leaving to see you, and he would thank you for being such a great friend.

EQ in Workplace Relationships

Imagine you are at work. You have a group project that you and your coworkers have been working on for the last month. The day before the project is to be submitted, you all realize that no-one worked on a specific portion of the project that was incredibly important, and without it, your project cannot be submitted. Each of you thought that part of the project was going to be completed by another person, and nobody checked on it until the day before it was due when you were all putting together the project so you could go over the final project. The final piece for the project is rather time-consuming.

With a lower EQ, you may explode on your coworkers. You may yell about it not being finished and assign blame to the other people around you, seeking any explanation that would remove blame from yourself. You say that it was clearly your coworker Mary's fault because she was supposed to do something else related to it. You may yell some words that are not appropriate in the workplace, and that causes you to get in trouble with HR. The assignment is never worked on. Further, you all are reprimanded for failing to complete the requirements, and you find yourself without a job due to the situation escalating so badly.

With a higher EQ, you may have been angry, and you may have seen the frustration on everyone else's faces, but instead of giving in to that anger and frustration, you instead chose to analyze the situation. You looked over what was still needed, and while it would be a lot for an individual person to complete, you point out that it is something that you can all finish relatively quickly if you each take a segment of it. Everyone in your group looks to you to hear you out, and soon, the mood seems to calm. Your coworkers follow your lead, and within a few hours, you all have completed the remaining work together. Your project is submitted on time, and everyone is thrilled with the outcome. You feel happy and fulfilled because you managed to turn a bad situation into a good one, and your coworkers feel as though you are trustworthy and like they can count on you when things get tough. The next time you all have a project, you are designated the leader who is in charge of making sure everyone has a role and that everything is being completed. This newfound admiration from coworkers betters your reputation with your bosses, and soon, you find yourself with a raise and promotion due to your tact and emotional intelligence.

EQ in Social Situations

Imagine you are at a big party. You have always been a bit more reserved and hate going to events like this, but you were pressured into going by one of your friends. The party is loud, obnoxious, and everyone around you is drinking, something you are not comfortable doing in public. One person walks by, clearly intoxicated, and trips and spills a beer right down your shirt. He slurs out an apology and continues on his way, leaving you drenched in beer in the middle of a party that you did not want to attend in the first place.

With lower EQ, you may look at your friend for a moment before exploding. You scream about how you did not want to attend the party in the first place. You tell your friend that next time, he should listen to you, and you throw down the drink you had been handed before storming out. Quickly, the party seems to quiet down as all eyes are on you. They watch as you leave, and the party seems to die down. Your friend awkwardly watches as you leave, and within the next few days, news of your outburst in the middle of the party spreads throughout your peers, tarnishing your reputation. People stop wanting to talk to you or invite you places, and the friend that you had yelled at seems less interested in continuing your friendship.

With a higher level of EQ, you may have stopped, been frustrated, but then recognized that it was an accident. You would not have allowed your prior annoyance at not wanting to be there to cause you to blow up. Instead, you would have quietly excused yourself to clean up without making a scene or destroying someone's flooring at a party.

You would have found something to do with your friend and tried to enjoy yourself, even if you would have rather been doing something else. By not being sucked into your anger, you are still able to find enjoyment in other things. You may even be able to make some new friends or try new things. Regardless of whether you eventually find something worthwhile, by not reacting volatilely, you are able to keep from overreacting and hurting people around you.

4

The Emotional Intelligence Framework

Emotional intelligence is composed of several different skills that make you capable of understanding and appraising emotions, regardless of whether they are your own or belonging to other people. People with higher EQ are typically much more effective at controlling and regulating their feelings, which enables individuals to better control behaviors.

Emotional intelligence is better understood by breaking it down beyond understanding what it is as a whole. The entirety of emotional intelligence is comprised of five separate realms of emotional intelligence, which are further organized into four quadrants that affect each other. Understanding these ways of breaking down and organizing emotional intelligence is useful in understanding where you stand and what the purpose of each of the skills is.

Realms of Emotional Intelligence

The skills of emotional intelligence can be broken down into five separate realms or behaviors and skills:

- *Understanding your emotions*
- *Regulating your emotions*
- *Keeping yourself motivated*
- *Understanding and recognizing the emotions of other people*
- *Managing relationships* (managing the emotions of other people)

Each of these realms of emotional intelligence is important, but being strong in one does not necessarily mean you are emotionally intelligent, nor does it mean that you will be particularly effective in social situations. In order to be emotionally intelligent, you must be proficient in all five realms. Someone who understands and controls his emotions with no regard for other people's emotions is not going to be emotionally intelligent; everything he does will be to ensure that his own needs are met. Likewise, someone who is skilled at understanding and recognizing other people's emotions but is awful at self-regulation of emotions is going to be selfless to a fault and find that her needs are never met. All five realms come together to create one well-rounded, emotionally intelligent person.

Quadrants of Emotional Intelligence

The four quadrants or domains of emotional intelligence are:

- *Self-Awareness*
- *Self-Management*
- *Social Awareness*
- *Relationship Management*

As you can see, each of these closely relates to one of the realms of emotional intelligence. Each of these skills can be sorted onto a chart to represent a different combination of self or social-relational and awareness or regulation.

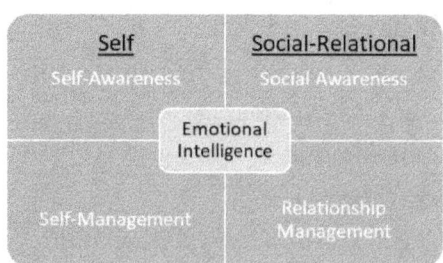

Each quadrant of emotional intelligence relates closely to the others. A high self-awareness typically lends itself to higher social awareness and self-management. When you have a higher social awareness and self-management, you are more likely to have stronger relationship management skills. When all four quadrants are strongly developed, that person is believed to be very emotionally intelligent.

Self-Awareness

Within emotional intelligence, self-awareness involves developing a deeper understanding of your own emotions. It involves knowing yourself and understanding what you are feeling or need. If you are able to identify and meet the needs of yourself, you are far more likely to be able to understand and meet the needs of other people. For this reason, the foundation of emotional intelligence begins with self-awareness.

Some traits associated with self-awareness include the following:

- Being self-confident because you understand yourself
- Being aware of your own strengths and weaknesses
- Being conscious of your current emotional state
- Understanding how your actions affect other people
- Understanding and being conscious of how other people or situations influence your own emotional state

By having a deep understanding of yourself, you have the foundation to understanding others. After all, if you could not identify when you are sad, how could you possibly hope to recognize sadness in another person? Without the most fundamental basics of emotions and how they impact you, you will struggle to ever truly relate to other people.

Low Self-Awareness

There are several signs that may point that you have a low self-awareness quotient. If you feel like you have any of these signs, you may need to work on your self-awareness.

- Easily stressed: When you are not in control of your emotions and not doing what is necessary to cope with the negative ones, you may find yourself easily stressed out by things that would not be a big deal to someone with a higher EQ. If you are not addressing your emotions as they come up due to a lack of knowledge to do so, you are going to see it build up and stress you out.
- Difficulty being assertive: People lacking the EQ necessary often struggle to handle conflict in a productive manner. Instead, they resort to passive or aggressive behavior to allow the conflict to pass.
- Struggle to describe emotional states: People who cannot label specific emotions as they feel them struggle to handle them. For example, while they may be able to identify that they feel bad, they cannot label whether what they are feeling is anxiety, frustration, or sadness.
- Operate on assumptions: People lacking in EQ often make a snap decision or assumption and then fall victim to the fallacy of confirmation bias; they will accept any evidence supporting their opinion while ignoring the evidence that contradicts it.
- Hold grudges: Grudges come from stress responses, and people lacking in EQ struggle to cope with that stress.
- Lock onto mistakes: People with lower EQs frequently lock onto their mistakes and refuse to look past them, or they forget about them, dooming them to repeat the same mistakes over and over again.
- Feeling misunderstood: People with lower EQs cannot clearly convey their own emotions because they do not understand them themselves, leaving plenty of room for misinterpretation.

- Lack of understanding what your emotional triggers are: Everyone has some sort of trigger—something that immediately causes strong, and often irrational responses to some sort of stimulus. Those lacking in EQ often do not know what theirs are.
- Hiding emotions: People with lower EQs tend to see negative emotions poorly and instead prefer to keep them hidden behind positive ones. This means that their needs are never being addressed because they are never using their negative emotions.
- Blaming others for how they make you feel: People with lower EQs see other people as responsible for triggering their own emotional responses instead of recognizing that no one is responsible for their emotional states.
- Being easily offended: Those with lower EQ typically lack the self-confidence those with higher EQs have. They also lack the understanding of their own strengths and weaknesses, which makes them a little more self-conscious when called out for them.

Self-Management

Self-management involves the ability to dictate your own thoughts, feelings, and behaviors. This quadrant of emotional intelligence focuses on your ability to manage yourself. It includes your responses to those around you and the situations you may find yourself in, as well as expressing your positive emotions while controlling negative reactions. While negative emotions are acceptable to feel, they should never be in control of you as a person. You should be able to manage feeling negative feelings while still not harming others or lashing out. It involves using self-awareness to keep those negative feelings within your control, as you are able to identify what they are and why you are feeling them.

Some of the frequently seen abilities in people with high self-management include:

- Keeping control of emotions: The ability to recognize and feel emotions without letting them dictate behaviors.

- Trustworthy: These people are reliable and often make it a point to follow through with what they have agreed to do.
- Flexible: The ability to roll with change when it is unexpectedly comes up without it ruining the plans or stopping the individual from meeting other goals.
- Optimistic: Negative feelings are not enough to discourage him or her from attempting to achieve desired results.
- Motivated to achieve goals: Knowing what is desired and motivated to make that happen.
- Willing to take initiative: Comfortable being the one initiating change and

Low Self-Management

- Struggle to control emotions: People with lower self-management struggle to keep their own feelings, and therefore their own actions, under control. They typically respond emotionally rather than rationally.
- Struggle to take criticisms: Anything negative said toward those with low self-management struggle to keep their disappointment or other negative emotions in control after feeling criticized.
- Cannot cope with change or the unexpected: Those with lower self-management struggle when things do not go according to plans. Coping with the change is difficult, as change or the unexpected typically come with stronger negative emotions.
- Impulsive: Those with lower self-management struggle to keep their impulses under control. When given the chance, they will take something that they like better, even if it has a worse consequence. The consequence does not matter nearly as much as the happiness from going along with the impulse.
- Need instant gratification: Oftentimes, people with lower self-management tend to go with gratification sooner rather than waiting for a better result. For example, they are likely to go

through with buying something they cannot afford with cash and put it on a credit card where they will pay significant amounts of interest if the alternative is waiting for months to be able to afford to pay cash. They'd rather have the item sooner, even if the consequence is worse.

Social Awareness

Social awareness focuses on understanding what other people want and need. It is the ability to look at someone else and understand how they feel or what they need in that particular moment. Those who are socially aware can tell at a glance how they should approach another person and how to keep situations calm. They oftentimes go out of their way to meet the needs of other people just because they feel as though they can, so they should. Oftentimes, they exhibit some of these traits:

- Empathetic: A deep understanding of how someone else feels and what is needed in the moment.
- An understanding of group structures: They recognize how society works and the idea of give-and-take communities in which everyone contributes something.
- Service-oriented: They prioritize other people's needs and wants in order to ensure that they are met as much as possible.

When you have a high level of social awareness, you are able to consider other people's wants and needs effectively and meet those needs quickly. These people frequently excel at being leaders or public speakers: They excel at speaking in the way that the people want to hear and use that skill to gain the support they need at their jobs. These people are typically quite charismatic, but also selfless in the sense that they are doing their best to ensure that others' needs are being considered. Social awareness requires a developed sense of self-awareness to really be effective.

Low Social Awareness

- Untrusting: Those who lack social awareness typically do not trust those around them, nor do they earn the trust of those around them. By never meeting other people's needs, they never establish themselves as trustworthy.
- Lack empathy: When lacking social awareness, it is quite difficult to understand what other people are feeling. They struggle to relate to other people meaningfully because they cannot deeply understand the other people's needs.
- Selfish: When social awareness and empathy do not play a role in life, people do not feel the pressure to ensure that other people's needs are met.
- Manipulative: Those without much social awareness do not feel bad about using other people in order to get what they want. Their lack of empathy means they do not care as much about hurting other people.
- Closed-minded: Social awareness allows for thoughts of diversity and understanding how every person, no matter how different, can contribute in some way. Those lacking in social awareness may not see the use of some people's skills or understand how nonessential jobs or skills may still contribute to the overall well-being of society.
- Isolated: Because those lacking social awareness do not trust others and lack sophisticated empathy, they typically retreat to be by themselves rather than associating with other people. They do not build up social support groups and instead live on their own.

Relationship Management

Relationship management is the most complex of the four quadrants of emotional intelligence. It involves the ability to influence other people through your own words and actions, allowing for inspiration, and the ability to mediate and solve conflicts that may arise within the

DEVELOPING EMOTIONAL INTELLIGENCE

groups you are inspiring. This is the ultimate trait for leaders: It is what enables you to lead effectively and kindly, earning that position as opposed to having to take it through domination. Those with high relationship management skills make conscious decisions about their interactions with others so they can get a desired outcome that best suits the needs at that moment.

1. **Make a decision** about the best way to proceed in the current situation. You have taken the time to analyze how those around you are feeling, as well as identifying the reasons for those feelings. From there, you will decide what the most effective ways to interact with those around you are, as well as considering the potential reactions you may get based on how you approach them. You will also consider how their reactions will affect you and have plans and skills in place to manage those potentially negative feelings effectively and appropriately.
2. **Interact with others** in the way that you have determined is the best possible course of actions. These interactions can vary in form. For example, it could be written or verbal, and with a single person or the entire group.
3. **Identify an outcome** you desire and tailor your interactions to that outcome. You will interact with the people in ways that you know will influence them to create the outcome you desire, adding an intentional element to the act of relationship management.
4. **Identify the needs** you are trying to meet in order to be sure that the outcome is the right one for the situation. You want your outcome to meet the needs of yourself, the people around you, or whatever the needs your decision is addressing are at that particular moment.

People with high skills in relationship management typically exhibit the following traits:

- Influential
- Inspirational
- Invested in the development of other people
- Willing to be the catalyst for changes
- Acting as the conflict mediator
- Cultivating and encouraging bonds between the people within the group
- Create teams that work well together and encourage teamwork or collaboration

Low Relationship Management

- Ineffective leader: Those who struggle with relationship management fail at being in leadership roles. They are typically too self-absorbed or socially blind to understand the nuances behind leading a group effectively
- Untrusted and disliked: Typically, those with low relationship management struggle to prove themselves trustworthy or likeable. People prefer to avoid them.
- Act selfishly: They may fail to acknowledge other people's needs, or simply do not care about others' needs for other reasons. Regardless, they do not inspire much loyalty when they refuse to help others.
- Are uninspiring: No matter how much they may ask other people to help them or do something, people do not feel motivated, obligated, or a desire to do as they were asked.
- Likely see a constant revolving door of new employees or relationships: Because these people struggle with relationships, they are frequently seeing new ones, either at work or in their personal lives. This constant refresh of people in the person's life mean he or she never really learns to develop meaningful relationships.

Interrelationship of Emotional Intelligence Components.
Within emotional intelligence, all four quadrants are interrelated. They build upon each other to create a well-rounded, emotionally intelligent individual. The basic foundation is formed by self-awareness; having a certain degree of self-awareness provides you with the ability to begin thinking about both self-management and social awareness. If you struggle with self-awareness, you are likely to struggle to move to the next step of self-management or social awareness. Oftentimes, self-awareness is one of the best places to begin practicing and strengthening your emotional intelligence, as the others require the skills developed through self-awareness to be effective at the others.

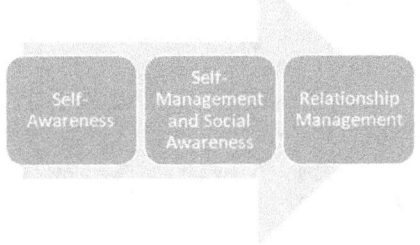

After self-awareness is developed, self-management and social awareness become possible. You cannot manage yourself and your emotions if you lack a basic understanding of what your emotions are or how they work, and likewise, if you are unaware of your own feelings, you cannot hope to understand how someone else is feeling or what they may need. Developing both self-management and social awareness leads to an ability to begin developing relationship management. Without self-awareness, the entire process of developing emotional intelligence becomes increasingly more difficult. It takes a mastery of self-awareness, self-management, and social awareness to begin to learn relationship management.

5

What is an Emotional Intelligence Test?

Imagine that you have just been fired from yet another job. You had always done your best at work but tried to keep to yourself. You did not care when people around you were struggling to complete their work, and even when you were free at that particular moment, you rarely extended an offer for work. Because you never developed many trusting relationships at work or went above and beyond, people were not particularly interested in helping you, either. One day, you were struggling to catch up on your work, and despite your best efforts, you could just not keep up. No one around you offered to help you, as you had never offered to help any of them, and eventually, you blew up at work. You could not take another moment of listening to two of your coworkers chattering right outside your cubicle, and in a moment of rage, you yelled at them to either make themselves useful and help you or get away from your desk. You may have even sprinkled in a few swears during your rant. Ultimately, you were fired and left wondering why, after all that time of you being a good employee who did the job and never caused trouble before, you were let go. Sure, you had one blow up, but everyone has a bad day sometimes, and that should have been excused considering your track record. This seemed to happen everywhere you went: You would go, do your job, keep to yourself, and ultimately be let go when you were doing your job regularly, and you could not understand why. Through some web searching, you found your answer: A lack of emotional intelligence.

You may be doing your job on a regular basis, but you have proven that you are not a team player in that particular situation. Workplaces want to build teams of people who work well together and will help each other when the need arises, not people who do the bare minimum to get their own work done while letting other people suffer the consequences of not having their work finished. With your newfound understanding of the value of emotional intelligence, you begin searching for how to improve it.

Ultimately, you feel lost. You may know that you struggle with anxiety sometimes, or that your ability to meet others' needs could use some work. Despite knowing this, you may have no idea where to begin or how to decide where to continue working on yourself. You know that you would like to be an emotionally intelligent person because emotionally intelligent people seem to do better in a wider range of situations, but are unsure of how to attain it or where you may need to improve yourself. Luckily for you, this is exactly why emotional intelligence tests exist!

Whether you want a general idea just for fun, or you are serious about understanding where you fall on the scale of emotional intelligence, taking a test can be a fantastic way to get that picture. While these may not always be accurate due to the way they are executed and because they rely on self-reporting of situations and moods, they still provide great general information that can point you in the right direction on your journey toward emotional intelligence.

Just as how IQ tests exist, there are also tests designed to quantify levels of emotional intelligence. These tests typically consist of several questions designed to assess your strengths and skills in emotional intelligence to create a hard number to represent your EQ. The tests can be crucial tools to understanding where your emotional strengths and weaknesses are, and can provide a more thorough understanding of yourself as an individual. These tests can come in a variety of forms, ranging from true or false questions, questions that ask you to quantify how much something describes you or the frequency of a behavior or can be verbal questions at an interview designed to gauge your emotional intelligence.

How EQ Is Tested

Typically, EQ is tested through a series of questions. You will be given a sort of quiz with a series of situations and circumstances, and you must identify how you would react or whether it describes you. The goal is for you to identify as honestly as possible to create the most accurate assessment that can be created. Each question created to test an individual's EQ creates a situation in which there are several reactions possible and assigns each possible reaction a score in relation to a specific quadrant of emotional intelligence. For example, a question testing self-awareness would likely question one's own reactions in certain situations regarding being stressed, overwhelmed, or otherwise negatively influenced by emotion, often in a way that can assign a value. For example, you may see a question that asks if you do not let your emotions get the best of you, with the choices you are provided being "always," "sometimes," "rarely," and "never." Always would score 4 points while never scored a 0. This allows for a quantifiable assessment of your ability to control your emotions.

The tests frequently ask a series of questions for each quadrant of emotional intelligence, and at the end, they add them up and divide the scores into several categories to use to provide your results. If you score in the top percentile, you are said to have high intelligence in that category, while average scores mean it could use some work, and low scores implying that you need serious effort in that particular category.

Together, you are able to add your questions together and see where you score.

Sometimes, workplaces will perform EQ tests during interviews when seeking to hire or promote people. In those cases, the test is most frequently done verbally, with an emphasis on understanding your own personal reactions to certain scenarios, or with you providing a time that you had a conflict at work and asking how you may have resolved it. You will often be given a question, and then allowed a few moments to consider it before being expected to answer it.

These questions typically relate to empathy or conflict resolution, and they are some of the most important questions at your interview. If your interviewer is asking you questions to judge emotional intelligence, then they are oftentimes specifically seeking out someone with emotional intelligence, even if that person is not the most qualified academically or experientially.

Why Test for EQ?

As discussed, emotional intelligence has a strong impact in virtually every aspect of your life. Understanding your EQ allows you to identify your strengths and weaknesses, which can be incredibly useful when it comes to recognizing your behaviors for what they are. You need to understand your weaknesses if you hope to compensate for them and begin to work on filling them in to prevent them from being problematic in the future. Your own relationships and general wellbeing will increase if you can raise your EQ, as you will become generally better at managing yourself and your emotional reactions. By bettering your control over yourself, you are able to avoid falling for the traps that many people do in communicating with others: Giving in to anger. You will be able to recognize your anger and use it to fuel your desire to fix the situation without lashing out or making the situation worse for yourself or others. You may find that your problem was a simple miscommunication, and someone who is emotionally intelligent can take that information and learn from it to ensure it is not a problem again in the future.

Beyond testing EQ to understand yourself, it is sometimes tested in other situations as well. Sometimes, interviews for jobs involve questions that test for emotional intelligence. It has been found that some of the best performing people in many different careers have higher EQs, even if they are less intellectually intelligent than some of the lesser-performing individuals. Ultimately, EQ has proven more accurate in determining success in workplaces than IQ.

Because high EQ is a better predictor of a good employee, many managers have begun using those questions to weed out people who are less emotionally intelligent and more likely to cause issues in the workplace. They ask questions that provide the hiring managers a better understanding of the interviewee's ability to recognize and regulate their own and others' emotions and behaviors, especially when needed to adapt to various workplace environments and situations. Employers want empathetic employees that are team players, great at communication, and well-equipped to handle a wide range of challenges or roadblocks that may be encountered during the work week.

Higher levels of social and emotional intelligence are important in a workplace, as those who are more emotionally intelligent place more of an emphasis on empathy, which means they will be there in support of their coworkers. If they see a coworker struggling, they are more likely to go forward and offer to help solve the problem than someone who does not see empathy as a major motivator. Those with higher emotional intelligence are also more in tune with their own strengths and weaknesses and are more receptive to feedback and constructive criticism than someone who struggles with their confidence.

What to Expect in an EQ Test

When taking an EQ test, you should expect to see a wide range of questions on various subjects. Some may be quite sensitive, such as asking about your own personal confidence levels, whereas others may seek to identify whether you are able to resolve conflicts or put other people's needs in front of your own. The tests are typically rather boring, and provide a series of similar questions, though they do have slightly different purposes for your score. You may see questions about your own emotions, as well as your interpretation of others emotions in similar circumstances, or you may seek questions that seek to measure how well you cope with the unexpected. Regardless of what the questions are, they all serve one purpose: To identify your weaknesses when it comes to emotional intelligence.

When you take a test, you must be honest. It is often helpful for people to go with their gut reactions when reading a question, as that gut reaction is typically the most accurate. Do not answer the test based on what you think may be the right or wrong answer, as all that will do is skew your data. If you want your test to be as accurate as possible and give you the most straightforward information about yourself, you must answer truthfully, even if you know it is an answer that would be attributed to a lower level of emotional intelligence. EQ is flexible and can be strengthened, so you should want the most accurate picture painted when taking the test. That accurate picture will be your roadmap to becoming more emotionally intelligent.

While the questions do not necessarily have to be taken in any specific amount of time, it helps to do them in one sitting if you can. You should be free of distractions when you begin your test, and you should make sure you have an ample amount of time free to tend to it. Some of the tests available can take up to an hour, though the one you will be provided in this book will be much shorter. You want to be able to focus on your questions within the same mindset and without other things distracting you that could potentially make you misunderstand the question or your own answer to it.

You should expect the questions to be easy enough to understand, though they may be about situations or traits about yourself that you have never considered. Give yourself a quick moment to consider them, and then write down the answer. Again, make sure that you provide your own honest answers to the questions rather than how someone else would answer for you. The important part is your own opinions and interpretations of yourself, especially because two of the quadrants are about yourself, and the basis of the entire emotional intelligence structure requires your own self-awareness.

Lastly, you should expect that this test will not be 100% accurate! As it relies wholly on self-reporting and involves questions on emotions, which are widely variable between people, you should take this as a general guide rather than as a diagnosis for what kind of person you are. It can absolutely point out your strengths and weaknesses, but you should make sure you take you understanding of the results as general assessments as opposed to being official assessments of your own emotional intelligence.

Sample Questions and Answers

The following questions and answers will be considered from the same hypothetical scenario introduced at the beginning of this chapter in which you imagine that you have been fired from your job after doing the bare minimum to meet your own job description without helping others at work and eventually having an outburst. Each question that will be provided will have an explanation of what it is testing for as well as the answer that the hypothetical you would provide, and what it would score if it were a part of this test.

Sample 1:

I am able to control myself when angry and keep myself from saying things I will later regret.

| 1. Never | 2. Rarely | 3. Sometimes | 4. Often | 5. Always |

You may have circled often here, with the reason being that oftentimes, you are able to control your anger. It is when you are already stressed out prior to being set off that you really struggle to control it and frequently say things in anger that you do not mean.

This question seeks to quantify self-management. It is asking you a question about your own feelings and your own behaviors to identify whether you are able to control yourself. One of the key facets of self-management is the ability to regulate your emotionally charged reactions, even when faced with the temptation to allow your emotions to rule you.

The answer never earns you 0 points, rarely earns 1, sometimes earns 2, often earns 3, and always earns 4 points toward emotional quotients. By answering that you can often control your anger, you earned 3 points toward your EQ.

Sample 2:
I understand what makes me angry most of the time.

| 1. Never | 2. Rarely | 3. Sometimes | 4. Often | 5. Always |

You may have looked at this question and circled 3. You know some of the things that make you angry, such as when you feel the pressure to perform at work, but sometimes, you do find yourself angry without knowing why, and you have noticed that it can cause issues in your relationships.

This question seeks to quantify self-awareness. It wants to identify whether you are aware of your emotions and if you understand what is causing them. Since self-awareness is all about understanding your emotions and what influences them in order to be able to develop the self-management necessary to control them, this is an easy way to get straight to the point.

Just as the previous question scored answers, an answer of never warranted 0 points, rarely earned 1, sometimes earned 2 points, often earned 3 points, and always earned 4 points. Your answer of sometimes earned you 2 points toward your EQ.

Sample 3:
People often look to me to lead group projects at work or school.

| 1. Never | 2. Rarely | 3. Sometimes | 4. Often | 5. Always |

Your answer here likely would have been 1. You never went out of your way to work with other people, nor did you ever try to assert yourself as a leader. You always did the bare minimum, and nobody in your workplace really trusted you since you never gave them a reason to do so.

This question sought to understand and quantify your relationship management skills. It wanted to identify whether you were often seen as a natural leader or if people naturally wanted to do as you said and follow your lead. Those with high relationship management skills are frequently seen as natural leaders in groups, and when they work in groups, people naturally want to do as the leader says because they do trust that person's judgment and know that he or she will do what is best for the team.

This question also uses the same scale of 4 points for always, 3 points for often, 2 points for sometimes, 1 point for rarely, and 0 for never. Your answer warranted a score of 0 in relationship management.

Sample 4:
I never concern myself with the welfare of others if it will be even a minor inconvenience to me to do so.

| 1. Always | 2. Often | 3. Sometimes | 4. Rarely | 5. Never |

After reading this question, you circled that you agreed with the statement. If helping others took away from your time at work or any free time you may have earned by finishing your work quickly, you would disregard the possibility of helping other people. You did not see a reason to do so, especially if it meant extra work for you that you would not be paid for.

This question sought to quantify your social awareness skills. This particular question was concerned with empathy and how much you showed for other people. Those with higher social awareness skills act empathetically, wanting to help other people, even if it is somewhat of an inconvenience. They do not mind helping out, so long as it is not directly harmful to them, and sometimes even when it is. Empathetic individuals will act selflessly for no reason other than they feel as though they should do so because they can understand and feel the other person's pain or stress.

This question changed the scoring pattern. In this instance answering always warranted a score of 0 often would earn a score of 1, sometimes earned a score of 2, rarely got a score of 3, and never earned a score of 4. Your answer assigned you a score of 0 for social awareness.

Ultimately, after taking your four scores from the four questions, you scored 5/16 in emotional intelligence. This is quite low and requires work in all quadrants based on the four questions answered.

6

Measuring Emotional Intelligence

Understanding that you can quantify your EQ is fantastic, but you need to understand more thoroughly how to judge what those scores mean. Why are certain scores important? How do they tell you what you need to know? Whenever you are testing something as abstract as emotional intelligence, it can be hard to really accurately quantify results. After all, the numbers used are going to be arbitrary based on whoever is executing the test. Some tests will have you answer out of 10 and provide you a score of 0-10 to decide how emotionally intelligent you are. Others will provide it out of 160. This book will have you ultimately calculate your score with a max of 40 points per quadrant, totaling 160 when your individual quadrants are added together.

How Emotional Intelligence Is Measured

As mentioned, your score will be measured out of 160 points. Each question you will answer in the next section can provide a minimum of 0 and a maximum of 4 points toward your quotient, just like in the sample questions that were discussed in the previous chapter. The questions that will be provided are carefully considered to analyze each of your four emotional intelligence domains. Each domain will involve 10 questions, providing a minimum score of 0 to a maximum score of 40. You will ultimately add up your scores after completing the questionnaire, and that is what you will use in order to identify what your EQ is.

When you have tallied up your score, you will want to compare it to the key that will be provided at the end. It will divide the possible scores into three different results that will tell you whether your score is low and requires attention to correct and develop it, effective, meaning that it is average, but could be strengthened, or enhanced, meaning you should utilize it to work on developing other quadrants that may be weaker or need work.

Remember, unless you somehow manage to score a perfect 160 on the test, there is always room for improvement. If you do not like the score you see in front of you after completing the assessment, you should use that displeasure as motivation to begin working on other aspects of yourself in order to better your emotional intelligence and strive toward a happier, more emotionally intelligent lifestyle.

At the end of the appraisal, you will be guided toward identifying your own personal weaknesses, as well as encouraged to work on the particular areas that are giving you a difficult time. You will learn where your weaknesses are through seeing your scores, and you will be given a baseline to work off of. Think of this first appraisal of your EQ as your pre-diet and workout weight and photos. This is where you are before you begin working to better yourself, and you should save it to look back on in the future after you have had time to dedicate toward growing your emotional intelligence. You may be surprised to see more growth than you initially expected, even after just a short time of working toward your goal of gaining a higher EQ.

How to Use Your Emotional Quotient to Understand Your Needs

Your EQ will be scaled into one of three categories: needing enrichment, proficient and functioning, or enhanced and strong. Understanding where each individual domain's EQ is will help you see where you are doing well and where you are struggling. If you know that you are struggling with self-awareness because you scored a 15/40, for example, you can use that knowledge to begin studying self-awareness. The last third of this book is dedicated to provide tips to improve emotional intelligence for each domain, and that is a fantastic first place to start improving yourself.

On the other hand, if you score 35/40 in self-awareness, but you have scored 12/40 in social awareness, you can use your skills in self-awareness to apply strengthening to social awareness. You already know plenty about your own emotions, needs, and how the world impacts them, so you can begin working to develop empathy skills instead. Your own self-awareness skills will be the foundation to bettering your social awareness.

When you learn where your domain skills fall, you are able to further understand your own behaviors as well. If you know that you have always struggled with managing your anger, for example, seeing that your self-management quotient score lowly may help you understand why and point you in the right direction to bettering yourself. You can meet that need to manage your own anger so it will no longer be overwhelming by following some of the practical tips toward bettering self-management. You will also be able to create concrete goals toward bettering your self-management and find guides to help you, step by step.

Ultimately, the most important way that knowing where your EQ sits on the scale is knowing your own weaknesses. One of the fundamental parts of emotional intelligence is having an understanding of your own weaknesses and developing them over time in order to compensate for that natural weakness. Because an EQ is not concrete or fixed, no matter which aspect is your weakest, you could theoretically work with it enough to make that weakness into your strongest domain. If you have always struggled with leadership but want to learn, that is a possibility, no matter what your temperament or current EQ. If your goal is to be highly emotionally intelligent with a strong relationship management quadrant, you can do that with the help of understanding where you are at now.

The Emotional Intelligence Scale

With many different methods to calculating emotional intelligence available throughout the world, it should come as no surprise that there are a multitude of scales available to judge that emotional intelligence as well. Each test is going to have a different scale that is used based on what is being measured.

The scale that this book will use is 40 points per quadrant with a max score of 160 for total EQ. Within this, scoring in the bottom 60% of any given category is seen as a weakness. Scoring between 60% and 85% is seen as being effective or proficient, but it could still be strengthened. Scoring in the top 15%, from 85% to 100% is seen as having enhanced or advanced levels of emotional intelligence. This higher level is incredibly tough to achieve naturally, but it can be consciously attained. See the following table for a basic breakdown of the results that will be used in this book's assessment.

Score	Individual Quadrant EQ	Combined EQ
Area for Enrichment: Needs work	0-24	0-96
Effective Functioning: Proficient, but could be strengthened	25-34	97-136
Enhanced: High EQ	35-40	137-160

Within this chart, you can identify the area for enrichment as a low EQ, effective function as average EQ, and enhanced as high EQ. People within these different scores may behave vastly differently due to the many different possible combinations of EQ. It is entirely possible to have someone that excels at both self-awareness and self-management but is poor at social awareness and relationship management. That person's score could potentially report as effective, or average, depending on how they scored. For example, assume you scored a 35/40 on both self-awareness and self-management, but only 22/40 on social awareness and 18/40 in relationship management. This person's social skills are quite low and needing improvement while self-centered skills are enhanced. This person's total EQ comes out to 110/160, which puts him firmly in the center of effective, or average EQ, though he cannot navigate a social situation for his life. While his total EQ may be acceptable, he is going to struggle with those low social scores. Despite these sort of outliers, EQ is still a generally effective way to look at emotional and social skills.

With an idea of what the scale looks like, it is time to look at some of the most common traits of people with both low and high EQ.

Low EQ Traits

People with lower EQ typically are much more volatile and less stable than those with average or high EQ. They oftentimes are very emotional and unpredictable, and while they may come across as passionate and spontaneous to some people, it is actually a sign of lacking the emotional intelligence necessary to be successful socially.

- *Lacking control over their emotions:* People who struggle with their EQ frequently are controlled by their emotions rather than being in control. This can lead to situations that are emotionally charged quickly, becoming worse as fuel is thrown on the proverbial fire.
- *Does not understand the feelings of others:* Because those with lower EQs typically struggle with empathy, they frequently come across as clueless about other people's thoughts, feelings, or needs, even if their feelings are clearly displayed on their expressions.
- *Lacking friendships, or failing to maintain them:* Those who struggle with EQ frequently also lack meaningful relationships

with friends due to not having the emotional intelligence necessary to maintain those relationships. Due to the volatile tempers of those with lower EQ and a lack of good problem-solving and conflict resolution skills, friendships rarely last.

- *Keeps a straight face:* Those who keep their faces blank at all time typically struggle to express their own emotions. This is often due to a lack of understanding how to express their own emotions, a crucial component of emotional intelligence, rather than a need or desire to keep their emotions shielded away.
- *May be emotionally inappropriate at times:* Because people with lower EQ tend to struggle with reading other people's emotions, they may behave inappropriately, such as making a joke at a funeral or talking about sexually explicit topics at a family-friendly party with children present.
- *Cannot identify emotion from tone of voice:* People who struggle with EQ frequently struggle to identify emotion from voice alone. While people with average or higher EQ are able to identify the emotion being conveyed by tone alone, people with lower EQ typically fail to do so.
- *Lacks sympathetic behaviors:* Both empathy and sympathy require sophisticated emotional intelligence skills that those without much EQ typically lack. Because both empathy and sympathy require the emotional states of another person to be understood, it can be a big struggle for those with lower EQ.
- *Emotional reactions are typically intense:* Along the lines of being unable to control their emotions, those with lower EQs typically react incredibly strongly or intensely, even when it is not necessarily warranted. If something is annoying, they become irate, or if they are happy about something small happening, they may be absolutely ecstatic. These extremes are felt due to a lack of emotional control to keep reactions at an appropriate level.
- *Does not respond emotionally to movies:* Oftentimes, we feel emotional attachments to characters we see on TV. In a love scene,

our feel-good hormones are pumping. In a tense horror scene, our own heartbeats quicken in response. These are empathetic responses with the characters in the movie or show, and someone lacking emotional intelligence is not likely to feel emotionally moved the same way as someone with a higher EQ.

- *Downplays the importance of emotions:* Almost as though they are in denial, oftentimes those who struggle with emotional intelligence typically try to downplay the importance of emotions and being able to communicate with them. They say that logic is more important, and lacking emotion is not nearly as much of an issue as lacking rationality. This is not true; however, as emotions and emotional intelligence are crucial to virtually every aspect of society.
- *Struggles with communication:* While the emotionally intelligent person is able to communicate tactfully, someone lacking a high EQ often resorts to name-calling, misdirection, and pushing the blame for situations onto the other person. This only serves to escalate the situation, rather than helping to deescalate it.

High EQ Traits

People with high EQ are typically much more adept at social situations than those with lower EQs. They are skilled at reading other people and juggling the needs of everyone, making sure that everybody is as satisfied as possible because of their own empathy. They are happiest when everyone else is content. These are some of the most common traits someone high on the EQ scale may exhibit:

- *Able to accurately name and describe a wide range of emotions:* Someone with high EQ is able to describe complex emotions beyond bad or good. They can say that they are feeling despondent or explain that they feel optimistically hopeful. Experts in

the field have found that only about 1/3 of people are capable of this.
- *Balances rationality with emotionality:* Emotions do not run the show, though they may influence it. People with high EQ are able to think rationally during emotional times, and they are able to use this skill to make good decisions, even during tough or distracting times or events.
- *Curious about others:* The curiosity of other people developed, regardless of whether you are actively interacting with that other person, is a byproduct of empathy. Because you are able to feel the emotional energy of other people, you become more curious about how others are doing.
- *Can regulate negative emotions:* While people with high EQ do not seek to avoid or quash any emotions they are feeling, they are able to regulate their reactions to them. Even when angry or scared, they are able to allow the rational part of their minds to control the situation. They never allow the negative emotions to overpower their rational thoughts.
- *Aware of strengths and weaknesses:* Because they are aware of themselves, they are able to recognize their strengths and weaknesses effectively and use that knowledge to prevent weaknesses from upsetting them or keeping them from succeeding. They are able to compensate for their weaknesses by using their strengths to their full advantage.
- *Good at judging other people's characters:* Because emotional intelligence is comprised mostly of social awareness, reading other people is a necessity. Those with high EQ have mastered this skill, and are able to make snap judgments about other people that are typically quite accurate.
- *Can manage toxic situations:* Because people with high EQs are able to control their own emotions and reactions, they are not fazed by the antics of toxic people. They are able to remain rational, which allows them to look at the situation empathetically to

look for some sort of compromise that allows for the toxic situation to be deescalated.
- *Understand that perfection is unattainable:* People with high EQs know that perfection is impossible and do not seek it out. They understand that they will fail sometimes, and understand that they will have negative emotions related to failing. They do not feel as though failure has to be avoided at all costs because they recognize that everyone fails sometimes.
- *Take personal time:* People with high EQ are masters at managing their own emotions and stress levels. They frequently take personal time to allow them to do so.
- *Has power over negative thoughts:* While everyone is bound to feel negatively and have negative thoughts sometimes, those with high EQ are able to shut that negative narrative down. They look at the situation rationally, disconnecting their thoughts from their feelings through mindfulness in order to keep from spiraling into a cycle of negativity.
- *Can communicate and resolve conflicts skillfully and tactfully:* Those with high EQ are capable of looking at other people's perspectives, even in arguments, and use that skill to resolve conflicts without allowing resentment to fester in relationships. Their communication skills are much more tactful than those with lower EQ, designed to keep the other person's perspective in mind while still conveying the message.
- *Resilient:* Those with high EQ are capable of rolling with the punches. Even in times of stress, they are able to react in emotionally intelligent ways. Someone who is afraid may be able to overcome their fear to protect their family or to save the life of somebody in danger because, even when emotions are running high, they are able to think about things rationally and separate their rational thoughts from the emotions that they are feeling.

Remember, most people do not fall solely into one category or the other. It is entirely possible to see a mixture of these traits or behaviors, though they tend to trend one way or the other. Someone with generally high emotional intelligence may have some of the low EQ traits and vice versa. People with average EQ are typically somewhere between the two extremes listed above. They may be generally decent at communicating and solving conflicts but may become a victim of their emotions, which could make it difficult to see clearly or rationally. Someone could be great at reading and meeting other people's needs but struggles to meet their own, instead choosing to sacrifice himself to meet the needs of other people. Someone incredibly emotionally intelligent may be great at communication and empathy but never responds emotionally to movies.

When trying to decide where on the spectrum someone falls, remember that almost everyone will have some low and high EQ traits. Very few people fall solely into the high EQ categories, and if they do, it is because of years of effort to strengthen their skills.

Now that you have made it through this chapter, try to identify where you think you might fall on the spectrum. Which of the high and low EQ traits do you notice that you exhibit? Do you think that your EQ is generally high, low, or average? Try to do this before moving on to the next section. The next chapter will be an assessment of your EQ, and it can be quite telling to predict where you may fall and see where you actually do. It can help you identify disconnects in your thoughts and behaviors and help you identify how accurate your self-awareness actually is.

7

Emotional Intelligence Self-Assessment

With your predictions for how you believe your own emotional intelligence levels will look, it is time to prepare to take the Emotional Intelligence Self-Assessment. You have learned all about emotional intelligence at this point and are ready to see where your own EQ stands so you can begin to work on strengthening it. You probably have a pretty good idea of your own strengths and weaknesses within the concept of emotional intelligence, but it is always helpful to see those strengths and weaknesses quantified in some sort of way to remove the abstractness from the concepts.

Instructions for this Assessment

Set aside some time where you can sit down uninterrupted for at least 20 minutes. You want to go somewhere relatively quiet and free of distractions. Turn off or mute any cell phones and make sure you are somewhere without television or music playing in order to actually focus on the questions given to you. Gather up a piece of paper or a word document on your computer and label it with numbers 1-10 for each category.

You will record your answer to each question as the number of the answer for future scoring. For example, if you choose answer 3. Sometimes as the answer to that particular question, you would record 3 on your scoresheet for future reference.

Remember, each question should be given proper consideration, and you should answer each question as honestly as possible. In order to ensure the most accuracy, you must consider each question and choose the answer that best suits you. You have a choice of 5 answers per question, and you should be able to identify one of them that works for you.

When you are answering questions, make sure you pay close attention to the order and scale of the answers. Sometimes, they ask for your agreement or disagreement, while other times, they ask how frequently you do something.

They sometimes flip with answer 1 being always some of the time while answer 1 can be never other times. You must answer the questions according to the scale provided in each individual question in order to ensure your results are accurate.

Now, without further ado, it is time to begin your assessment!

DEVELOPING EMOTIONAL INTELLIGENCE

1. I frequently feel nervous or anxious about situations I am in, and I am frequently unsure why I am feeling the way I do.

   | 1. Always | 2. Often | 3. Sometimes | 4. Rarely | 5. Never |

2. I typically try to avoid negative or troubling topics because they make me feel bad.

   | 1. Always | 2. Often | 3. Sometimes | 4. Rarely | 5. Never |

3. My negative thoughts typically spiral out of control, and I struggle to reign them in. As soon as they start, they seem to have a mind of their own.

   | 1. Always | 2. Often | 3. Sometimes | 4. Rarely | 5. Never |

4. I am very stubborn or hard-headed and have a difficult time admitting to being wrong or taking fault.

   | 1. Always | 2. Often | 3. Sometimes | 4. Rarely | 5. Never |

5. I am able to motivate myself to complete difficult or unpleasant tasks, even if I do not want to do them.

   | 1. Never | 2. Rarely | 3. Sometimes | 4. Often | 5. Always |

6. I can be civil and polite to someone that I dislike if there is a situation that requires me to do so, such as at a business meeting or during a family event.

   | 1. Never | 2. Rarely | 3. Sometimes | 4. Often | 5. Always |

7. I frequently hide my true emotions or feelings from others because ultimately, emotions are unimportant when trying to act in a rational manner.

   | 1. Always | 2. Often | 3. Sometimes | 4. Rarely | 5. Never |

8. I am comfortable handling unexpected roadblocks that I encounter in life, such as a minor car accident, or being laid off from a job.

   | 1. Never | 2. Rarely | 3. Sometimes | 4. Often | 5. Always |

9. I am able to point out the good things in life that balance out the negative, even in bleak situations or times that are dark.

   | 1. Never | 2. Rarely | 3. Sometimes | 4. Often | 5. Always |

10. I am able to identify my emotions and accurately label and convey those feelings with words in ways that other people can easily understand (for example, telling someone that you feel anxious and agitated instead of saying that you feel bad).

    | 1. Never | 2. Rarely | 3. Sometimes | 4. Often | 5. Always |

SELF-AWARENESS

1. I make sure I adjust my behavior to reflect who I am interacting with (for example, speaking professionally and politely with my coworkers while speaking much more casually and joking around with my friends).

1. Never	2. Rarely	3. Sometimes	4. Often	5. Always

2. If I can tell that someone I am interacting with is feeling uncomfortable or intimated by me, I attempt to change my own behavior in order to make him/her feel more relaxed (for example, making a few jokes, lightening the tone, or adjusting body language).

1. Never	2. Rarely	3. Sometimes	4. Often	5. Always

3. When I am feeling anxious or afraid, I am able to calm myself down and regulate my feelings rather than falling victim to negative thoughts.

1. Never	2. Rarely	3. Sometimes	4. Often	5. Always

4. I struggle to make decisions in periods of emotional turmoil and freeze up in emergencies or other tense situations.

1. Always	2. Often	3. Sometimes	4. Rarely	5. Never

5. I know exactly what role I can play on a team and how my own strengths can be valuable assets, and I can convey that message clearly and efficiently.

1. Never	2. Rarely	3. Sometimes	4. Often	5. Always

6. I am always looking for ways to improve myself and strengthen my skills. Self-improvement is never finished, and there are always different ways to improve, even when you may not feel like it.

1. Disagree completely	2. Disagree somewhat	3. Neither agree nor disagree	4. Agree somewhat	5. Agree completely

7. When I notice my emotions that I am feeling, I am able to accurately convey why I am feeling the way that I am, even if the cause of the emotion is somewhat obscure (for example, feeling sad on an anniversary of a bad event, or being reminded of grief because you saw something that reminded you of someone you lost).

1. Never	2. Rarely	3. Sometimes	4. Often	5. Always

8. I feel the need to consult other people before making emotional decisions.

1. Always	2. Often	3. Sometimes	4. Rarely	5. Never

9. I struggle with expressing myself when things get emotional and tend to shut down as opposed to open up in times of need or in stressful situations.

1. Always	2. Often	3. Sometimes	4. Rarely	5. Never

10. When I feel as though I am stressed out, and life is overwhelming, I feel as though I should give up.

1. Agree completely	2. Agree somewhat	3. Neither agree nor disagree	4. Disagree somewhat	5. Disagree completely

SELF-MANAGEMENT

DEVELOPING EMOTIONAL INTELLIGENCE

1. When arguing with someone, I typically seek to compromise in order to end the conflict without either of us feeling as though we are the loser.

   | 1. Never | 2. Rarely | 3. Sometimes | 4. Often | 5. Always |

2. I find it difficult to take a look at someone else and understand how they are feeling by body language alone.

   | 1. Agree completely | 2. Agree somewhat | 3. Neither agree nor disagree | 4. Disagree somewhat | 5. Disagree completely |

3. Listening to people discuss their opinions that differ from my own is upsetting for me, and I struggle to see why they would think the way they do (For example, on topics surrounding politics or religion).

   | 1. Agree completely | 2. Agree somewhat | 3. Neither agree nor disagree | 4. Disagree somewhat | 5. Disagree completely |

4. When discussing something with someone else who seems to have a more basic vocabulary, I often try to adjust my own speech without commenting on the other person's capabilities to match the other person's level for optimal communication. I want the other person to understand me, even if that means simplifying my own speech beyond what I normally would do.

   | 1. Disagree completely | 2. Disagree somewhat | 3. Neither agree nor disagree | 4. Agree somewhat | 5. Agree completely |

5. I have no problems upselling someone a product that I know they do not need if it will better suit my own production or earn me a better commission, even though it will cost them money.

   | 1. Agree completely | 2. Agree somewhat | 3. Neither agree nor disagree | 4. Disagree somewhat | 5. Disagree completely |

6. I am careful to word things in ways that I know are the least offensive in order to get my point across effectively and tactfully. I care about how other people are feeling and do not want to offend them.

   | 1. Never | 2. Rarely | 3. Sometimes | 4. Often | 5. Always |

7. I am adept at handling toxic or high-conflict situations without letting emotions get the best of me. By making it a point to understand the toxic person's position, I am often able to find an answer that does not leave one person walking away entirely dissatisfied.

   | 1. Disagree completely | 2. Disagree somewhat | 3. Neither agree nor disagree | 4. Agree somewhat | 5. Agree completely |

8. I am frequently the voice of reason within my group of friends, and they frequently come to me during emotional periods for support.

   | 1. Never | 2. Rarely | 3. Sometimes | 4. Often | 5. Always |

9. Seeing other people unhappy or hurt genuinely upsets me and motivates me to try to help them in any way that I can.

   | 1. Disagree completely | 2. Disagree somewhat | 3. Neither agree nor disagree | 4. Agree somewhat | 5. Agree completely |

10. I always consider how my own behaviors influence those around me when deciding the best course of action.

    | 1. Disagree completely | 2. Disagree somewhat | 3. Neither agree nor disagree | 4. Agree somewhat | 5. Agree completely |

SOCIAL AWARENESS

1. I am able to motivate change in other people, both good and bad. People often look to me as inspiration and seek me out for advice on how to proceed in difficult or emotional situations because I have established myself as capable of being able to navigate through those difficult situations without allowing emotions to cloud my judgment.

1. Disagree completely	2. Disagree somewhat	3. Neither agree nor disagree	4. Agree somewhat	5. Agree completely

2. I can handle emotionally stressful or volatile situations calmly and can function rationally during emergencies, even when feeling intense emotions at the same time.

1. Disagree completely	2. Disagree somewhat	3. Neither agree nor disagree	4. Agree somewhat	5. Agree completely

3. I naturally fall into leadership roles during group projects at work and school due to my ability to recognize and juggle all of the members' unique needs, strengths, and struggles while balancing them with the need to complete the project.

1. Never	2. Rarely	3. Sometimes	4. Often	5. Always

4. I can recognize that sometimes, the best course of action is to change, and I am not afraid to be the person that triggers or initiates the change, especially if those around me are hesitant to do so.

1. Never	2. Rarely	3. Sometimes	4. Often	5. Always

5. I can identify the strengths and weaknesses of people around me, as well as the ways that the other people can build upon their strengths and work to strengthening their weaknesses in order to better themselves, and I can tactfully provide the feedback and criticism necessary to inspire the betterment of those around me without offending them.

1. Disagree completely	2. Disagree somewhat	3. Neither agree nor disagree	4. Agree somewhat	5. Agree completely

6. People often feel inspired to do what I want them to do and frequently agree to do whatever I ask of them because of the way I go about asking for it. I am generally described as influential and charismatic.

1. Disagree completely	2. Disagree somewhat	3. Neither agree nor disagree	4. Agree somewhat	5. Agree completely

7. I am considered trustworthy by most people I meet, and because of that trustworthiness, I am often able to foster a sense of teamwork within other people if I encourage it.

1. Disagree completely	2. Disagree somewhat	3. Neither agree nor disagree	4. Agree somewhat	5. Agree completely

8. I can listen to a disagreement between two people and carefully consider both positions before explaining each view in a tactful manner that allows the other person to better understand the opposing viewpoint, enabling me to quickly and efficiently solve disagreements between other people and calm the situation.

1. Disagree completely	2. Disagree somewhat	3. Neither agree nor disagree	4. Agree somewhat	5. Agree completely

9. People often describe me as inspirational and say that my charisma and social skills frequently encourage those working with me to do their best work. My own eagerness to complete the task and create a positive workplace environment triggers others to want to do the same.

1. Disagree completely	2. Disagree somewhat	3. Neither agree nor disagree	4. Agree somewhat	5. Agree completely

10. Because I am an excellent judge of character, I can typically identify people's strengths and weaknesses and use that information to create teams of people that work well together and bring out the best in each other.

1. Disagree completely	2. Disagree somewhat	3. Neither agree nor disagree	4. Agree somewhat	5. Agree completely

RELATIONSHIP MANAGEMENT

Calculating Your Scores

Congratulations! You have completed the questionnaire. That was the hardest part of this process. From here, your next step is to begin calculating your EQ, both in individual quadrants and as a whole.

The simplest way to do this is to add up the answers you got in each quadrant and subtract 10. The answers were designed, so every 1 was worth 0 points while every 5 was worth 4. The EQ score is calculated by taking the number of the answer you chose (let's say x for ease of understanding) and subtracting 1. So the equation on an individual level is x-1= total EQ points per question with x being the number of the answer you chose. You can calculate it out by doing that for each individual score and then adding it all up at the end, or you can shortcut by simply subtracting 10 from the entire sum.

This means that your quadrant score is calculated by adding up all of the answers within that quadrant and subtracting 10. When you have your four-quadrant scores, you can add them together to get a total EQ score as well as to get an idea of how well-rounded you are.

Remember to record both your quadrant and total EQs so you can begin to understand your score. Now that you have your scores recorded, it is time to begin interpreting each individual score!

Your Results

Remember the table provided for you in the previous chapter that told you what to expect in terms of the scale this test will use? It is time to refer to that again. For ease of access, the table will be repeated here. This is the same table that was shown before with no changes made. It shows you how your score should be interpreted. In any given individual quadrant, a score of less than 24 means that area needs work to bring it up to functional. A score above 35 means that that particular skill is quite developed and you should consider it a strength, with anything between 24 and 35 being effective. It does the job, but is not necessarily strong and has room for improvement.

Score	Individual Quadrant EQ	Combined EQ
Area for Enrichment: Needs work	0-24	0-96
Effective Functioning: Proficient, but could be strengthened	25-34	97-136
Enhanced: High EQ	35-40	137-160

With this table, identify which ranges your EQ falls into and see the following categories for understanding what this means for you.

Low EQ (0-24 individual quadrant or 0-96 total points)

With lower EQ, you often struggle with emotions and social situations in general. You are not in control of yourself or your life, and your emotions rule you. This frequently pushes other people away and makes understanding other people's communications with you quite difficult. You are easily offended and easily triggered into negative emotions.

You do not feel very good about yourself, and you may be very aware of how you never seem to quite mesh with people in social settings. You struggle with relationships of all kinds, and no matter how often you may try, you fail to better the relationships. You cannot help the urge to yell during arguments or disagreements, and because you cannot work through your emotions, people tend to avoid you.

You are ultimately likely incredibly unhappy in your life. You are frequently, or sometimes always, frustrated, feeling as though no one is understanding you without realizing that no one is understanding you because you are not communicating effectively. This only exacerbates your negative emotions as you are not only feeling upset or angry, but you are also further angered or upset because no one seems to understand the base feelings and you are unable to communicate them.

If you scored in this category, you have plenty of work to do to get yourself up to par emotionally. Scores in the low EQ range *require* further attention, or they will continue to be a detriment to you.

Average EQ (25-34 individual quadrant or 97-136 total points)

People with an average EQ are fully functional members of society. If you scored within an average range, you typically get along with others well enough, though there may be some conflicts here and there that can create bumps in your relationships. While you like yourself more than someone with low EQ, you still recognize that you sometimes struggle with your emotions. You are able to control them when they are not particularly strong, but when you begin to get overwhelmed, you may lose that control you have. You may hurt your relationships sometimes, but you are also able to recognize when you do so and work to repair them.

You are willing to take responsibility for your actions if they cause problems in other areas in your life, but it typically happens after you have had the time to cool down and recognize that you said or did something that you wish you may not have. You may struggle to let go of mistakes that you or others make, and you may hold grudges.

While you are able to navigate social relationships well enough, they are frequently bumpy, and you still find yourself struggling from time to time. You wish that you were better at your relationships and that you could change who you are. You wish that you were better at managing your own emotions, especially during times of stress when you *know* that those are the most important times to have control of your emotions. Despite knowing that, you struggle.

If you have scored in this category, you are emotionally intelligent enough to get by and not fail at every social situation you have, but you still feel the struggle of acknowledging and managing both your own and other people's emotions, and that struggle can lead to feelings of unease and unhappiness, while also contributing to feelings of anxiety and stress. You should consider strengthening the quadrants that scored within this range, building upon the skills you already have, in order to feel more secure and established. The better your emotional intelligence, the more secure and successful you will feel, and the more successful your relationships will be.

High EQ (35-40 individual quadrant or 137-160 total points)

Congratulations! You scored as having high EQ in one or several categories! This means that you are quite emotionally intelligent. You are in tune with your own emotions and understand how they influence yourself and those around you, and you have also developed the ability to control and regulate your emotions, so they do not dictate your actions. You are true to who you are and have a solid idea of your identity, values, and beliefs, and you will act in ways that line up with them.

While you are also aware of your own emotions, you are able to recognize the emotions in other people as well. You are skilled identifying the emotions and needs of those around you and are able to juggle both their and your emotions. You are likely extremely empathetic, enabling you to navigate through complex relationships while also influencing and managing other people's emotions and actions. You are likely a natural leader, charismatic and charming, and people frequently seek you out or choose to follow you.

You are enjoyable to be around in a wide range of emotional contexts, and people want to continue relationships with you. You are good at managing conflicts and defusing tense situations, which makes you effective in leadership roles. You are mature and willing to take jokes flung your way, even if they are deprecating.

You are likely flexible and go with the flow. It takes a lot to shake you or break your confidence, and most of the time, you are able to work with even the most difficult of unforeseen circumstances.

If you have scored highly in any of your emotional intelligence quadrants, you should use the skills you have in order to strengthen weaker quadrants in order to bring your total EQ up to this category. If all of your scores fall within this category, there is still work you can do to further develop and maintain your skills! Do not feel as though just entering this category is enough to warrant giving up on developing your skills. Seek to identify your weakest quadrant and start trying to bring it up to the same level as the highest.

What Now?

With your understanding of your scores, you are ready to move on to the next step: Strengthening your EQ! You now know what your strengths and weaknesses are, and with that in mind, you can focus on the relevant sections in the next part of this book. Part III will provide 50 practical tips for each realm of emotional intelligence to help you begin to better your own EQ.

Remember, no one is ever done working on their EQ. Even if you score highly, you can still learn from the tips provided in the next section of the book. Practical advice can teach you new ways you may not have considered before to practice and maintain your EQ. Even those with high EQ levels will begin to lose those skills if they do not maintain them, and even those with high EQ levels are not perfect. Everyone has weaknesses that they should strive to reinforce to better themselves.

8

50 Practical Tips to Improve Self-Awareness

1. **Take time to reflect on emotions:** Every day, you should sit down and reflect on how you felt during the day. Think about how you responded to various situations, and name the emotion that was felt during that response, with particular focus on negative emotions. For example, if you feel as though your spouse is holding you to unfair expectations, how do you respond? How do you respond when a friend confronts you on something that you did that hurt his feelings? You need to be able to identify how you react in the moment to eventually begin to build up self-management.
2. **Keep an emotions journal:** Every day, write down the strongest emotions you felt throughout the day and reflect upon them. What made you feel that way? What was happening when you felt the way you did? Do you see any patterns?
3. **Be observant about your own current emotions:** Always be aware of how you are feeling in the moment. If you are stressed, acknowledge that. If you are sad, acknowledge that as well. You need to get in the habit of checking in with yourself to see how you are feeling if you hope to recognize your emotions in a meaningful way.
4. **Ask others about how you act:** Sometimes, getting feedback from other people is crucial to understanding how you are portraying yourself. This can offer you valuable feedback about

whether you are communicating your own emotions and needs effectively, or whether you need to continue working on conveying how you are feeling in the moment.

5. **Practice pausing before reacting:** It is easy to react in the moment when emotions run high. You need to get in the habit of pausing, taking a deep breath, and deciding on what you will say or do next. By giving yourself that moment, you can identify when something you wanted to say would not be conducive to bettering the situation.

6. **Ask yourself why you feel the way you do in the moment:** A large part of self-awareness involves understanding your feelings, including why you are feeling the way you are. You must be able to stop and analyze your feelings, including identifying why you feel the way you do if you hope to be in control of your emotions when you move on to self-management.

7. **Ask yourself what you can learn from criticism:** Criticism can be tough to hear if you already have low self-esteem. If you are not very emotionally intelligent, you may struggle regulating your disappointment when someone voices their criticism of you, but asking yourself whether that criticism could be beneficial to you allows you to make that criticism constructive instead of destructive.

8. **Ask yourself what you can learn from failure:** Like criticism, understanding what you can learn from failure to avoid repeating it in the future is important. If you learn from your mistakes, you will grow, whereas if you simply avoid trying again, you have stunted yourself.

9. **Practice using more descriptive vocabulary about emotions in general:** When you feel sad, are you despondent? Disappointed? Ashamed? Fragile? Lonely? Learn to be more specific than sad, happy, angry, or other blanket emotions. This could be the perfect time to open up a thesaurus and widen your vocabulary.

10. **Always name every emotion to yourself as you feel the strong ones:** When you are feeling particularly emotional, make it a point to identify it. Putting a name to the emotion helps you understand what you are feeling, and also may help you regain control of the situation.
11. **Vocalize your emotions when talking to people you are close with and pay attention to how your voice changes based on your feelings:** People's voices change based on their emotions. You can hear the emotional crack in someone full of despair, or the harshness of the tongue when enraged. Listen to how your own voice changes when you are feeling a range of emotions.
12. **Practice pushing yourself out of your comfort zone:** No one likes being uncomfortable, but sometimes, you need to push yourself to get it over with. Just as sometimes, it is better to rip off the bandage, it can be better to force yourself into uncomfortable situations so you can learn to manage them. Be realistic with this step and slowly work yourself into uncomfortable situations as opposed to throwing yourself deep into your emotional triggers.
13. **Identify your emotional triggers:** Speaking of emotional triggers, learn to identify yours. You need to understand the things that are most likely to set you off so you can be prepared when you notice one of your triggers nearby and begin to rein in your reactions.
14. **Do not discourage or judge your feelings as they occur:** Good or bad, and you should allow you to feel your entire range of emotions. Just because you acknowledge them and feel them does not mean that you are a slave to them.
15. **Avoid making important decisions when in a bad mood:** Making decisions in a bad mood can lead to impulsive choices that you regret later. Reserve decision making for when you are calm.
16. **Avoid making important decisions in a good mood:** Similar to making choices when in a bad mood, making them in a good

mood can also sway you to take risks you would otherwise be uncomfortable with.
17. **Check in with yourself during stressful situations and identify your emotions in that moment:** Especially when you notice that you are stressed out, you should check in with yourself. Identify how you feel in the moment and use that feedback to adjust your behaviors accordingly.
18. **Attempt to identify emotions of characters in the media:** Since a big part of being emotionally intelligent involves identifying emotions, try to practice identifying the emotions of other people as well. This is beginning to bridge your self-awareness skills to social awareness.
19. **Practice identifying expressions either online or with a trusted friend:** Make expressions related to various feelings and see if your friend can identify yours. This can give you an idea of whether you are communicating your emotions clearly or not.
20. **Pay attention to what happens in your body during emotional events:** When you are feeling high levels of emotion, pay attention to how your body feels and the body language you exhibit. If you are happy, are you smiling with a relaxed body? If angry, are you tense with your fists clenched or your arms crossed?
21. **Recognize that negative emotions are important and useful:** Negative emotions should not be avoided. They need to be embraced and understood if you hope to be an emotionally intelligent individual. You must be able to read a wide range of emotions, including the negative ones. They serve their purposes just as much as the positive emotions and deserve that recognition.
22. **Look for patterns in your emotional reactions:** Similar to the act of identifying triggers, and you should also identify patterns in all forms of emotional reactions. Identify what makes you a certain way by making a mental or physical note of what preceded the emotional reaction. Eventually, you may begin seeing patterns

in which feeling supported leads to you being happy and relaxed, or being busy tends to flare up your stress and anger responses.

23. **Practice mindfulness:** Mindfulness is the act of separating your actions from your emotions and allowing the emotions to occur while you observe them. Take a back seat and let your emotions free while you attempt to analyze them from a detached perspective. This may provide valuable insight to what is causing your reactions.

24. **Stop treating your emotions as good or bad and start acknowledging them for what they are:** Emotions all serve important purposes, and assigning them a normative value devalues them. You need to recognize that you are feeling your emotion for a reason, regardless of whether it is good or bad. You should not seek to avoid negative emotions, but rather to understand and utilize the negative emotions felt to respond appropriately to the situation.

25. **Become comfortable in your discomfort:** You need to learn to not shy away from your discomfort. As much as you may want to avoid it, learning to acknowledge and accept your discomfort is a surefire way to being able to control your own emotions. You must be okay with being in discomfort if you hope to be able to strengthen your self-motivation later on in the process of strengthening your emotional intelligence.

26. **Identify your values:** Understanding what you value is the first step in understanding what is motivating your behaviors. Take the time to acknowledge and identify the things you value most. This could be family, relationships, money, success, fame, reputation, or anything else.

27. **Identify how your values influence your behaviors:** Once you understand what your values are, take the time to notice how those values affect your behaviors. Do you act in ways that are conducive to your values? If not, how can you fix your behaviors to ensure that your values and behaviors line up? You will be

much happier without that sort of cognitive dissonance in your life.

28. **Create life visions based around your values and decide where you would like to be in the next five years:** With your understanding of your behaviors and your values, identify where you would like to be in five years. This should line up with your values, so if what you value beyond everything else is family, it may be related to your own marital and parental status. If you value success, you may decide that you want to achieve a promotion or two during that period.

29. **Learn your stress cues:** What do you do when you are stressed? Do you withdraw or become aggressive and agitated? How do you respond physically to stress? Does it make you nauseous or leave you itching for a fight? Do you lash out or shut down?

30. **Observe how your emotions seem to spread through your entire body and the effects they have:** Emotions are contagious, and while they may start in the mind, they quickly impact the rest of your body as well. Happiness may leave you relaxed and refreshed while anger leaves you feeling physically stressed.

31. **Constantly pay close attention to your own reactions and emotional states, even when they are primarily positive:** You need to learn to identify your emotions, both positive and negative and identify how they make your body feel. Pay attention to your breathing, heart rate, and body language and begin to label the physical reactions with the emotions felt.

32. **Create a regret letter:** Addressing this to yourself at a younger age, write down what you regret doing so far. Apologize to yourself for making the mistakes you feel are particularly pressing, such as skipping out on an opportunity to attend a school you really wanted to for a lackluster reason. This acknowledges your own failures without making excuses for them. You are able to practice addressing your own shortcomings to yourself, which is a low-risk situation.

33. **The funeral test:** In this activity, you should sit down and write your own eulogy. You should answer questions about yourself, such as how you would like to be spoken of at your funeral, what you want to be remembered for, and how people will think of you when you are gone, compared to how you think people would currently answer. This allows you to see, more or less, where you are now compared to where you want to be and allows you to further understand where you may need to make changes in life to make up for past mistakes.
34. **Write your most important tasks down daily:** Start each day asking yourself what you must accomplish during the day to reach your long-term goals. If your long-term goal is to strengthen your ability to read your own emotions, perhaps you write down three activities you will do for the day to reach that goal. This helps you identify your values and goals while giving you a clear-cut list that will guide your behaviors, even when your emotions may be trying to lead you astray.
35. **Practice apologizing:** No matter how painful you may find it, make it a point to apologize for any mistakes you have made, or if someone comes up to tell you that you did something to hurt them. Make your apologies meaningful as well: Identify what you did in the apology and promise to try to avoid doing it in the future. Even if you may not have felt like it was a big deal, you need to recognize how your own emotions or behaviors influenced other people.
36. **Practice grounding techniques when feeling stressed or overwhelmed:** Grounding techniques can help you stop and identify how you are feeling in that moment. It brings back your awareness of your current state and allows you to act wisely.
37. **Question assumptions:** If you find yourself reacting to assumptions you have made about other people or their behavior, ask yourself why you made the assumption in the first place and analyze its validity.

38. **Trust your intuition:** We make snap judgments for a reason. Trusting your intuition is different from responding emotionally. Trust your intuitive judgments without allowing your emotions to rule the situation.
39. **Listen to your inner monologue:** When learning to track your emotions, allow your inner monologue to go uninterrupted while paying special attention to your train of thought. It can provide valuable information about why you feel the way you do.
40. **Tell yourself 'no':** Teaching yourself to refuse some instant gratification can teach you to control your impulses. Make it a point to tell yourself no to at least five different small temptations a day, whether they are a beer; time wasted watching cat videos or other junk food.
41. **Hold yourself accountable:** Acknowledge when you make mistakes and make it a point to tell yourself what you can do differently next time to avoid repeating them.
42. **Stop the excuses:** If you have made a mistake, do not make any excuses. Similar to holding yourself accountable, you should make it a point to own your mistakes and do not try to minimize or downplay them in any way, no matter how badly you think it will reflect on you.
43. **Stop gut reactions:** When lacking self-awareness, you run on auto-pilot and allow emotions to rule, responding with gut reactions. You need to stop those gut reactions in the act, or preferably before they happen.
44. **Avoid negative self-talk:** Do not talk down to yourself. This can lead to stress and anxiety and should be avoided. There is enough negativity in the world without you adding more toward yourself.
45. **Learn about body language and use it to fix your own:** Use biology to your benefit and take poses that naturally encourage hormones and confidence, such as standing straight up. Learn to

mimic people that can communicate charismatically and effectively, such as hand gestures.
46. **Understand your personality type:** Take a personality test and identify whether you are an introvert or extrovert. It will explain an awful lot about your behavior if you understand what kind of person you are.
47. **Meditation:** Practicing meditation teaches you to get better at relaxing your body and focusing on your breathing. You will also learn how to keep your mind on track when it begins to wander.
48. **Identify strengths and weaknesses:** Consider what your greatest strengths and weaknesses are. Understanding these will make you more self-aware and allow you to utilize them where they can be beneficial.
49. **Acknowledge you are not perfect:** By accepting and acknowledging that you are not perfect, you alleviate the fear of failing. Failure is inherently human, and when you acknowledge that, failing becomes infinitely less frightening.
50. **Monitor progress:** Track where you are before you start trying to strengthen your self-awareness. Look at your EQ score and compare it to where you are a month or even a year from starting. See how it has changed.

9

50 Practical Tips to Improve Self-Management

1. **Breathing practice:** In moments of stress or high emotions, remember to regulate your own breathing. Be aware of how your breathing changes when you are stressed or angry and make it a point to regulate your breathing to control your mood. After a few deep breaths, you may find yourself feeling calmer and more in control of the situation.
2. **Weighing emotion vs. rationality:** Consider the pros and cons of responding to a high-risk situation with emotion and rationality. Is it something that requires passion and emotion, such as deciding whether to propose to someone? Or is it a situation that requires logic, such as deciding how much house you can afford with your current income? By being able to step back and weigh the benefits of responding emotionally and rationally, you will begin to see a clearer picture of the situation at hand.
3. **Make goals known to those around you:** By making your goals publically known, you force yourself to be accountable for those goals. People will have expectations that you will meet them, and may even help you in the process of achieving your goals, which also asking as deadlines loom closer. What better way to kick yourself in gear than to make your goal known to others, especially when it is a goal that directly affects them?
4. **Take a moment to count to 10 before responding:** When you are feeling emotional in a situation, take a few seconds to take in

a deep breath and count to ten in your head. This allows the moment of emotion to pass and keeps you from reacting with negative emotions. You can instead respond with something that will benefit everyone.

5. **Take a night before you decide on important choices:** It can be easy to want to respond with emotion when facing a big decision. Rather than making those decisions based on emotional gut reactions, give yourself a night to mull over the decision and allow the most intense emotions to pass.
6. **Talk to people who are skilled at self-management:** Get advice from people around you that are good at managing their own emotions. Those people may be able to provide you with their own tips and tricks to managing their emotions!
7. **Take the time to smile more:** Our bodies often respond with emotion to physical stimuli, and if you smile, you can improve your emotional outlook. Make it a point to smile and feel your entire emotional state begin to slowly shift to a positive one.
8. **Make time daily for problem-solving:** Schedule in a time that allows you to address the day's problems tactfully. This way, if you run into a complication during the day, you know there will be time to address it later if it can wait, and it becomes less stressful.
9. **Control your inner monologue:** It is hard to be outwardly positive and in control of your negative emotions when they are running rampant in your mind. Make sure that you control your thoughts and keep them away from negativity. Use the skills developed in self-awareness, such as meditation, to keep your mind on track.
10. **Drown out negative thoughts with positive ones to keep yourself motivated:** Challenge yourself to come up with two positive thoughts every time you have a negative one. This drowns out the negativity and allows you to see positives that you may not have considered otherwise.

11. **Visualize what success looks like for you:** Create a picture in your mind that you are working toward. Decide exactly what you want it to look. This is what you will seek to create with yourself and provides motivation. You know what success looks like and will be able to clearly identify your goal.
12. **Plan the steps necessary to achieve that success and act toward them:** Begin to plan out the steps that you will need to take to achieve your goal. If you want to be a more reliable friend, make it a point to plan out what a reliable friend will look like and what steps you need to take to make that happen, such as always following through with what you promise.
13. **Engage in self-care:** Make sure you maintain yourself. Take the time to exercise, eat healthily, and do something for yourself to alleviate stress levels. When your stress levels are lower, it is generally easier to control your negative reactions.
14. **Focus on your skills and abilities rather than on what you cannot do:** If you focus on the negative, your entire mindset will remain negative. Rather than dwelling on what you cannot do in a situation, instead focus your attention on what you can do instead.
15. **Make it a point to take away something valuable from every encounter:** There is something valuable to learn within every single encounter, whether it is how your own body language or tone affected another person or how you responded in a certain situation. Make it a point to find something valuable in encounters, especially if you feel as though the encounter was pointless.
16. **Schedule in time for yourself to relax:** You need to keep your stress at a manageable level if you hope to be effective at managing your emotions.
17. **Recognize that you can strengthen these skills, and your current abilities are not your permanent limitations:** Your self-management skills are not inherent or fixed. Remind yourself that you can influence them, for better or for worse.

18. **Make a plan for handling your negative emotions when they occur:** If you struggle to react well in certain situations, try to make yourself contingency plans that will help you mitigate negative behaviors or thoughts. By having a plan, you will have something to fall back on if the stress is too much.
19. **Work on rewarding patience and discouraging instant gratification:** You want to avoid being impulsive or making decisions solely based on emotion. Try to reward yourself when you were patient and rational about a situation.
20. **Make it a point to control your emotions using body language:** Use your body language to influence your emotions. If you are keeping your body in a relaxed pose, your mind is more likely to follow through than if you are actively preparing for a fight.
21. **Show people around you that you are listening and attentive with positive body language:** Practice using your body language to convey that you are attentive to other people. You can communicate an awful lot just through facial expression.
22. **Make plans to manage your stress levels:** When stress begins to get to be overwhelming, create plans to bring it back to a manageable level. Perhaps you could break down whatever task you are working on into smaller steps, or take a break from the work altogether if that is an option.
23. **Create a good work-life balance that is tolerable:** You need an appropriate amount of time to yourself to enjoy with your friends and family, and if you want to keep your stress levels down, you will find a balance between the work you have to do and being there for your loved ones.
24. **Eliminate toxicity and negativity wherever appropriate:** Just because you can deal with the toxicity and negativity does not mean that it is not draining. Remove things that bring you nothing but negativity. Without the constant negativity, you may be blown away by how much easier it is to manage your emotions.

DEVELOPING EMOTIONAL INTELLIGENCE

25. **Imagine a wide variety of different circumstances and predict how you will react within each:** This is similar to planning out how you will handle negative emotions, but with a twist. You are to play out how the variety of scenarios will go and predict your own reactions and results, as well as how changing your reactions may impact the results. This is more of a thought experiment than planning out your actions.
26. **Break your routine to get yourself out of an emotional funk:** If you feel as though you are stuck in an emotional rut, you can kick yourself out of it by changing your routine. By doing something new and unpredictable, your body does not have a natural, habitual response, and you will be able to do a sort of emotional reset.
27. **Create a schedule that you adhere to** While this may seem counterintuitive after the previous suggestion, remember that schedules keep things manageable. If you are juggling a lot, setting a schedule with strict times at which you rest, work, problem solve, take time to yourself, and fit in anything else you need to, you will be able to better manage your needs. Having needs met means your emotions are easier to control.
28. **Remind yourself that you are in control of your actions:** No one makes you do anything. Only you can choose to do what you are doing. Keep this in mind the next time you are slipping into negative actions.
29. **Remind yourself that emotions are fleeting:** Remind yourself that your emotion is temporary and fickle. They are impacted by everything, and just because you feel one way at that moment does not mean it is appropriate to act upon it.
30. **Remind yourself that emotions are nothing more than your brain trying to process data:** By reminding yourself that emotions are simply data and not actions or orders, you remove the control over yourself from them. You recognize that the emotions are only as powerful as you let them be.

31. **Treat others fairly and with respect:** Remember to treat those around you kindly and fairly. You should treat them the way you would like to be treated. Yes, the kindergarten golden rule still applies in adulthood, even for people you dislike.
32. **Always keep your word in order to develop trust with other people:** In order to establish yourself as trustworthy, make it a point to always follow through with what you say you will do. Not only is this an excellent exercise in self-control, it also sets the stage for social awareness and relationship management.
33. **Always look for learning experiences, even in mistakes or mishaps:** Even if you mess something up, seek to learn from the mistake. Understand what you did wrong and learn from that to ensure you do not repeat it in the future. Sometimes, the best way to learn is to fail and face the consequences.
34. **Challenge yourself regularly:** Do not allow yourself to fall into complacency and comfort. You should always be seeking to better yourself and hone your social skills, especially if you want to have good leadership or relationship skills.
35. **Always ask yourself how the other people feel in various situations:** Practicing empathy in real time can be particularly useful in helping you manage your own behaviors. If you can see that your behaviors are hurting other people, you are more likely to rein in those behaviors in order to avoid inflicting that pain.
36. **Encourage adaptability or flexibility through spontaneity:** While routine is important, you do not want to become too rigid. Sometimes, spontaneity is the perfect way to practice your flexibility skills. You can challenge a friend to come up with an entire day's worth of activities with no input from you to see how you respond to the surprises and lack of a plan.
37. **Continue to work with self-awareness techniques:** Do not forget your prior skills that you practiced in self-awareness just because you have begun focusing on self-management. Remember to continue practicing labeling your own emotions in real time,

DEVELOPING EMOTIONAL INTELLIGENCE

while also applying them with empathy and seeing how other people are responding to your emotions.

38. **Recognize the separation between yourself and your emotions:** Remember, just because you feel emotions does not mean that you *are* your emotions. You can feel angry, sad, or even foolish or weak, without defining yourself. Do not allow your emotions to define you. Instead see them for what they are: Your current emotional state and nothing more.

39. **Pick your battles:** Even when something is bothering you, only push the point or challenge it if you feel like it is worthwhile. Sometimes, it is not worth the trouble to correct something or be bothered by something someone said. Only pick battles that you feel strongly about.

40. **Let the little things go:** Along with picking your battles carefully, know when it is okay to let things go. Sometimes, you have to agree to disagree and walk away from an argument for everyone's sake, and that is okay. Knowing when it is that time is a fantastic example of self-management skills.

41. **Choose how you want to respond to a situation and stick to it:** Is this a situation in which you want to be defensive? Offensive to protect your beliefs? Should you be doubtful of your actions? Or is this a situation in which you need empathy or self-awareness? Choose which of the responses you need and try to stick to it.

42. **Ask for feedback from others around you:** After handling an emotionally volatile situation, try asking someone who was nearby, but not involved in the situation actively, how they felt it was handled, particularly in regards to your own feelings. Make sure that you are open to hearing the potential criticism that you will receive in return.

43. **Ask yourself how you would feel toward someone else behaving the way you are:** Take a moment to reverse the roles in your mind. How would you feel if the other person were treating you

the way you are treating them? If you feel as though you would be comfortable with it, then you are probably handling the situation well, whereas if you would be bothered, you may want to correct some of your behaviors.

44. **Practice communicating clearly in ways that are not offensive and are tactful:** Even when you may feel tempted to say something that you know is rude, and even if you feel as though that rudeness might be justified, try to find better ways to convey your point that are not offensive. This shows self-restraint, which is important when you are trying to manage your emotions.

45. **Celebrate your successes:** While you have learned that you should make sure you treat failures and mistakes as learning experiences, you should also recognize successes as worthy of celebration.

46. **Listen to what others are saying and do not interrupt:** Especially in situations in which someone else is complaining to you, make it a point not to interrupt. Even if you feel as though the problem is that person's fault in the first place if accusing them of failing is going to worsen the situation, simply provide an attentive ear. Pay attention to the other person's cues before providing your own feedback, and if you will be calling them out, make sure it is done in a tactful manner.

47. **Remember that positive attracts positive:** Just as ruminating on negative thoughts can continue to spiral your mood down, your own positive thoughts can become infectious as well. If you are generally behaving positively, you own emotions will better the moods of yourself and those around you.

48. **Choose productive actions**: If you choose to behave productively, you will find yourself feeling positively in general. It may be easy to slip into old habits or to choose gratification over productivity, but remember, you will be happier and less stressed if you ensure that your work is done before your time that you use for yourself.

49. **Seek advice from someone who is not currently emotionally invested in your situation:** This allows you to see someone else's perspective on a problem that you may have tried to solve but found that your methods were not very effective. You also may get feedback you never considered, such as one of your actions coming across as inflammatory.
50. **Remember that this is a process:** Recognize that there is never an end to learning how to self-manage. No matter how good you are at it, you are never going to be perfect. There will always be room to improve.

10

50 Practical Tips to Improve Social Awareness

1. **Make it a point to learn the name of everyone you regularly interact with:** This small step means that you have taken the time to acknowledge other people and you are willing to show them that they are important. This shows them that you acknowledge their existence and recognize them as individuals.
2. **Be mindful of your body language as you go through your day:** By presenting yourself as open and relaxed, people around you will feel more at ease, especially if they have to come up to you to speak or interact for any reason.
3. **Understand the importance of timing when delivering unpleasant news:** Knowing when to mention problems is almost as important as knowing how to break bad news. If you time what you are saying just right, you minimize the risk of upsetting the other person.
4. **Have icebreaker questions planned to break the awkward silence:** Have some sort of conversation topic you can use during those awkward silences that tend to happen at the most inopportune moments. The other person will likely appreciate having the silence filled, and you may even manage to make a friend with a new person.
5. **Be attentive during meetings or interviews:** Especially during meetings and interviews, you should be focused on the other peo-

ple in your group. Make sure that you are always showing signs of attentiveness, such as making eye contact and nodding your head.

6. **Always prepare for social gatherings:** When you know, you will be at a social event, make sure you have a few basic conversation topics to fall back on and that you have considered the setting, mood, and type of event. You would not wear a suit to a football game, and likewise, you should not go to a causal birthday party expecting to speak about the most recent problem at work.
7. **Be in the moment with people you interact with:** Really give people you are talking to your undivided attention. Show them that they are valued and important to you when you are speaking to them. This strengthens relationships and also encourages more empathy and understanding.
8. **Identify the feelings of people out and about, even if they are strangers:** Take a day to people walk and identify how people may be feeling based solely on their body language. You can tell a lot based on how someone is behaving and holding themselves, and this is an excellent exercise in practicing being able to read someone else.
9. **Practice how to listen effectively:** Make sure that you are really hearing the other person, rather than pretending to listen while really thinking about other things or doing something else. Giving undivided attention to someone shows respect and acknowledgement.
10. **Understand and accept differences and diversity:** Welcome that some people have different opinions, and that is okay. Even if you and your coworker do not agree, recognize that diversity allows for broader opinions.
11. **Practice empathy:** Make it a point to understand how those around you are feeling. Really feel what they feel, relating to them on a more personal level and use that to strengthen relationships.
12. **Try to see the bigger picture in your interactions:** What is the context of your interaction? Why are you having the conversation

that you are? Is this important or conducive to the atmosphere of the group? Consider all of this.

13. **Identify the mood in the social setting:** What is the general mood of the group at this moment? Is it somber? Why? Is it more lighthearted? How are people behaving? These types of questions will help you develop a deeper understanding of those around you.

14. **Observe how your words impact other people and learn from the reactions of others:** This is important to understanding how to communicate. You should be able to tell at a glance how other people are understanding your words. If they seem to be shying away from your words or tone, it may be time to reconsider your methods.

15. **Ask follow-up questions to develop a deeper understanding of what the other person is saying:** When you are listening to another person, make sure you ask questions about what is being said to not only show that you are listening but also to develop a deeper understanding.

16. **Change your tone to match the setting or audience:** Some people require different tones. You should speak to children differently than your coworkers, and people at a party differently than people grieving at a funeral. Knowing how to adjust your behavior based on situation shows that you understand emotional intelligence.

17. **Remind yourself that not everyone has the same experiences or worldview as you:** Just because you have a deeply held belief does not mean that other people share that belief. Other people may have had the opposite experience or may have developed different worldviews that directly contradict yours. Recognize that they have every right to their opinion in the same way that you do.

18. **Pay attention to small details and quirks of those around you:** If you notice that people have routines that they follow, you will

be able to notice when they do not follow that routine, which can cue you to double check that everything is okay.

19. **Especially in workplaces, do not interrupt people:** When you are listening, do not cut other people off to change the subject or argue. Your job is to listen well until it is your turn to talk.

20. **Maintain gentle eye contact while talking with other people:** By maintaining eye contact, you are cuing the other person that you are actively listening, and by making sure that eye contact is gentle and friendly, you are conveying that you are not a threat.

21. **Always apologize when it is warranted, and even if you have unintentionally insulted someone:** Being able to put aside your pride and apologize to someone else shows that you value and respect the other person's opinion and feelings. Even if what you are apologizing was not intended to be hurtful, you are acknowledging the other person's feelings as valid.

22. **Keep your cell phone or computer off or closed during social interactions, barring actual emergencies:** When you are interacting with someone else, make it a point to give them undivided attention. Do not make them compete with your phone or your computer. You should ideally have both put away out of sight when interacting with other people.

23. **Ask guiding questions:** When you are trying to understand a dynamic, situation, or another person's emotional state, especially relating to a conflict, asking guiding questions can get you the information that has not been provided that you need to proceed. By guiding the conversation, you may be able to fix the conflict.

24. **Repeat back what was said to you worded slightly differently to confirm you understand:** Yet another skill related to good listening, by repeating back what you heard, you not only cue that you listened to the other person, but also that you understood them as well.

25. **Do not take notes during meetings or interviews:** Note-taking is important in college when there are vast amounts of informa-

tion to absorb, but in meetings, you are expected to contribute. Instead of focusing on taking notes, you should focus on developing a working understanding of the material through interactions.

26. **Help people when they seem stressed or overwhelmed:** Going back to empathy, you should seek to help other people just because they are stressed out. By doing so, you help ensure their needs are met and strengthen your relationship with them.

27. **Take a genuine interest in other people:** Be interested in what the people around you are doing, even if it something you personally do not care for. While you may not enjoy writing, you can still be interested in your coworker working on a novel and cheer for her when it is completed.

28. **Take a genuine interest in the welfare of the people around you and be willing to intervene if you can help:** Related to the prior step, taking an interest in the welfare of others can build rapport with other people. People are more inclined to like you and trust you if you help them.

29. **Do not be afraid to suggest something new in a situation that is not working:** Social awareness involves being aware of how you can influence others, and that sometimes includes triggering change. Suggest a new perspective when you have a situation that is failing. It might be a perspective that has gone unconsidered until the.

30. **Always put the needs of the group ahead of the needs of yourself:** Because social awareness involves empathy and taking care of the group, there is no room for selfishness. You need to put the group ahead of yourself sometimes for the betterment of the entire group, and you need to know when to do that.

31. **Be honest in how you respond when asked, even if the honest response may be unwanted:** When someone asks you for feedback, you need to ensure that you provide it honestly and

thoughtfully. Even though sometimes, you may have to share an unpopular opinion, you should be free to share your thoughts.

32. **Communicate with tactful language:** By keeping your language tactful and neutral, you will be able to explain difficult or unwanted topics in a way that minimizes hurt or emotional harm. This is what doctors call bedside manner, and it is helpful in far more situations than just medical settings.
33. **Acknowledge the skills of other people:** Being able to look at other people and recognize their own skills and strengths takes empathy and social awareness. By acknowledging the other person's skills, you may be able to find ways that those skills can benefit everyone.
34. **Provide other people feedback to help them develop who they are:** Being able to see people's weaknesses is also important, as is being able to point out ways that those weaknesses could be patched up to keep them from becoming too detrimental in the future.
35. **Limit or eliminate social media for a week or two:** We often spend far too much time obsessing over our social media, and it comes at a cost of empathy and isolation. By forcing yourself to step back, you will further foster actual human interaction instead of staring at a screen.
36. **Begin networking and meeting new people:** One of the easiest ways of developing social awareness is to go out and meet new people from all sorts of backgrounds. Meet people with new or different worldviews or people who are in different professions. You never know when you might meet someone who can help you in the future.
37. **Avoid voicing complaints:** If you want to bolster your social awareness, you need to avoid voicing too many complaints. Those complaints can bring the general atmosphere of the social interaction down as well as paint yourself as a victim that cannot fix the situation you are complaining about.

DEVELOPING EMOTIONAL INTELLIGENCE

38. **Avoid causing drama, or allowing other people to cause you drama:** Along with avoiding complaints, you should seek to avoid drama. People, by and large, do not enjoy dealing with drama, and they will go out of their way to avoid it. Likewise, you should not allow other people the ability to influence you so strongly that they create drama for you.
39. **Try to keep your speech and general demeanor positive:** Positivity is infectious, and if you are able to keep your own speech and demeanor positive, you will see the positivity of the entire social setting increase.
40. **Avoid giving in to peer pressure, especially if whatever others are pressuring you into is something you do not agree with:** When you are in social settings, you may feel pressure to do things that you are not comfortable with. You should not feel as though you have to sacrifice your own values for other people, especially if you disagree with them.
41. **Toe the line between helpful and overly critical:** It is important to be able to provide constructive criticism, but that criticism can quickly become negative and overbearing if you are not careful. You must be mindful to keep your criticism helpful without sugar coating it while making sure that what you are saying is still constructive.
42. **Do not dwell on the past, especially regarding what other people may have done to you:** Being able to recognize that the past is in the past and forgive others for mistakes, especially when those mistakes where truly mistakes and not intentional, you are recognizing the humanity in other people. You are recognizing and accepting that people are not perfect and sometimes make mistakes. This keeps you out of the negative grudge trap.
43. **Join social groups with people who share similar interests as you:** Further extrapolating on the importance of social interaction in order to develop social awareness, try to find groups outside of your comfort zone who share similar interests. You may

be pleasantly surprised at the new kinds of people you can meet by joining clubs or groups in your area, and your social skills will thank you for it.

44. **Compromise when there are conflicts:** Recognize that there is no way for everyone to walk away from a conflict entirely happy. The best you can do is offer up compromises where each person gets some of what they need. Identifying conflicts and the compromises that can solve the conflict requires higher levels of emotional intelligence.

45. **Find some sort of common ground between yourself and the other person:** When you find yourself interacting with someone who seems entirely foreign to you, seeking out some sort of common ground is the perfect way to relate to each other. This can be anything from a common hobby or taste in music, or even as simple as having a sibling that is the same age. By connecting to someone when you first feel that connection is impossible, you are using your social awareness.

46. **Pay attention to how closely people orient themselves to other people:** Be aware of the physical distances between people. Those who are uncomfortable with one another typically keep a larger physical distance between them than people who are comfortable. This can be an important part of body language.

47. **Volunteer and get involved in your community:** This suggestion sees you getting involved in your community while also helping meet needs that would otherwise go unmet. This is the perfect way to practice your empathy and skills involving understanding diversity.

48. **Observe how people naturally respond to you and respond to those reactions:** You can tailor your own body language and communication skills to situations by watching how other people seem to react to you. This empathy makes you appear to be very emotionally intelligent.

49. **Use mindfulness to look past emotions and get a better understanding of the situations at hand:** When you are in an emotionally charged situation, remembering to step back with mindfulness to reevaluate the situation can help you see where a disconnect may be. Perhaps something you have said is insensitive. Knowing where you went wrong will enable you to correct for it.
50. **Continue to practice self-awareness and self-management to better your social awareness:** Remember, all of your emotional intelligence skills build upon each other. You need to maintain all of them to be a well-rounded individual.

11

50 Practical Tips to Improve Relationship Management

1. **Be open-minded:** You should be willing to consider anything anyone suggests to you without feeling strong emotions either way toward the suggestion. By being open-minded, people will not feel judged when they come to you with problems, suggestions, or other conversation topics. They will feel as though they can trust you, and that trust will go a long way.
2. **Enhance and deepen your communication:** Find your way of communicating and enhance it to make it as effective as possible. If you know that you like to make compliment sandwiches to deliver criticism, for example, master the art of tactfully explaining parts that need work.
3. **Communicate clearly:** Always be as clear as possible when communicating. Seek to use specific language that is difficult to mix up or misunderstand. Words that lack ambiguity will be your best friend when trying to communicate clearly and effectively.
4. **Ask if others have any questions for you:** Always encourage those you are working with to ask questions after you finish explaining something. This enables them to mull over the material you have provided while also showing that you value them and their understanding.
5. **Remember to pay attention to details:** Small details in relationships and communication matter! Recognize even the smallest

and most insignificant of strengths and weaknesses, as you never know when they will be relevant to your projects.

6. **Be welcoming to feedback:** Always welcome criticism, no matter how harsh, and make sure those you work closely with understand this. When you are provided with feedback, make sure you thank the other person for it and make it clear that you mean it. If you are gracious about receiving feedback, even when it is negative, you are more likely to get honest feedback in the future.

7. **Be trusted:** Do everything you can to establish yourself as a trustworthy individual within your social and workplace groups. By being trustworthy, people are more likely to be swayed by your words because you have never steered them wrong before.

8. **Be the person anyone can talk to about anything:** An open door policy harbors further trust and makes people feel as though they can approach you without fear of judgment.

9. **Don't try to avoid what will happen anyway:** If the inevitable is something you would rather not deal with, it is better to get it over with quickly. This shows your social circles that you are not afraid to approach uncomfortable or undesirable situations quickly and with tact.

10. **Acknowledge the feelings of those within your groups:** This leaves all members of your group feeling validated, which in turn lends itself to creating a group of people more inclined to help you or follow your lead.

11. **Be a complementary person:** Always seek to insert yourself into situations that you know your own skills complement. If you are good at organization while another person is good at research, the two of you have skills that complement each other, and you could be valuable assets to each other.

12. **Be a complimentary person:** Yes, this is different from #11! Compliment people on a job well done. This acknowledgment of their skills and success will make those around you feel recognized and valued.

13. **Show that you care:** Little tokens of appreciation, such as a hand-written thank you note or a birthday card, let those around you know that you value them as individuals and strengthens your relationship with them.
14. **Be decisive:** Do not be afraid to make a decision, especially when others seem to be struggling with the task of doing so.
15. **Explain why you make decisions:** Along with being willing to make the decision, you should have the tact and communication skills to explain to those around you why you made the decision you did.
16. **Be able to provide direct, constructive feedback:** You should be able to quickly and tactfully identify and suggest areas that those around you need to improve, with those suggestions developed after time spent getting to know the individual.
17. **Make sure your intention and impact are in sync:** Saying the wrong thing with the right intentions is just as harmful as saying the wrong thing with the wrong intentions. Make sure that when you are wording something, especially if it is negative or a criticism, that you word it in a way that is constructive and cannot be misconstrued negatively.
18. **When addressing a challenge, offer a solution to it:** The solution should be something that you see as a potential fix to the problem! This points the other person in the right direction.
19. **Be able to handle tough or uncomfortable conversations with tact:** Do not shy away from difficult subjects. People will appreciate you more if you discuss things tactfully and directly.
20. **Set boundaries:** You should develop your own boundaries and enforce them. This lets other people know just how far they can go with certain things before you have a problem.
21. **Respect boundaries other people set:** Complementary to your own boundaries, you should try to recognize the boundaries that other people set and enforce.

22. **Assume people mean the best, even when things don't work out:** Try not to be offended if someone struggles to communicate and bungles the message. Instead, assume they meant the best and move on with life. There's no use to clinging to negativity.
23. **Volunteer for uncomfortable leadership roles:** There is no better way to start practicing your relationship management skills than taking a leadership role. Even if you feel out of your element, give it a shot.
24. **Be willing to question status quo:** Do not be afraid to challenge how things are being done and suggest new ways to try things out.
25. **Offer advice and opportunities to help other people grow:** Whenever you are working with other people, offer ways that they could further enhance their skills, or even suggest that they try something new.
26. **Earn the loyalty of other people through your own actions:** Those with high relationship management quotas win the backing of people through their behaviors. You should make it clear that you are worthy of that loyalty by always seeking to help other people.
27. **Prove yourself trustworthy:** Always follow through with what you say you will do so people around you know they can count on you to help them when they need it.
28. **Be able to identify ways that other people can work together:** Especially if you are a leader in a group, try to pair up people who seem to work well with each other, whose skills balance out the weaknesses of the other person and vice versa.
29. **Learn to to quickly identify and deescalate conflict within groups:** Try to watch for rising tensions so you can deescalate them before they blow up. This will further earn trust as you manage to stop conflicts in their tracks
30. **Give every member of your group a task that allows each to be productive in their own ways:** Being able to identify the dif-

DEVELOPING EMOTIONAL INTELLIGENCE

ferent strengths people bring to the table celebrates diversity and develops trust that you are seeing a bigger picture.

31. **Be able to talk someone down from high emotions quickly and efficiently:** Learning this skill means that you have mastered the art of influencing other people's emotions. Other people may feel like you always have the right words for every situation.

32. **Develop the ability to relate to other people easily:** If you can relate to anyone quickly and easily, you are able to better empathize with them quickly, and they will be more inclined to listen to an empathetic person.

33. **Be grateful when someone shows an act of kindness toward you:** You should always show that you appreciate those around you, especially if they show an act of kindness. Send them a note thanking them or tell them in person.

34. **Ask yourself what you can do for the people you believe can help you too:** Before asking yourself what other people can do for you, you should first ask how you can benefit each other. Relationships should be mutually beneficial.

35. **Always ask for what you want:** The worst that can happen is someone says no. By always asking for what you want, you are clearly stating your desires, and those who agree or align their desires with you will be able to do so.

36. **Always try to create win-win situations:** Situations should create the best possible solution for as many people as possible. A situation in which one person is on top while everyone else suffers is not conducive to a team environment and should be avoided.

37. **Find ways to create a team identity:** Your team should be more concerned with a group identity and success than individual success. If you want to have higher relationship management skills, you should foster this through team-building exercises and rewarding them for group successes.

38. **Foster bonds within the team:** Along with a team identity, creating bonds within the teams encourages people to work with

each other and genuinely enjoy doing so rather than seeing each other as inconveniences.

39. **Always show up a few minutes early:** To be on time is to be late, and is incredibly disrespectful. Instead, you should always aim to be at least 5 minutes early. This shows that you value the other person's time.
40. **Treat everyone you meet, no matter what they look like or how they act, as incredibly important:** Basic human decency says we all deserve the same basic consideration, and you should remember to acknowledge this.
41. **Under-promise so you can over-deliver:** This is a sort of work-around to managing expectations. If you promise to have something done by Friday to give yourself extra time, you can return the project by Tuesday and win brownie points for having it done three days early.
42. **Work with your peers' strengths and weaknesses:** When working with others, make sure you insert yourself in areas that you believe you will be the most effective and useful at complementing everyone else. This shows them that you are seriously considering their abilities and recognizing them on individual levels.
43. **Accommodate other people whenever you can:** Empathy allows for compassion, and by accommodating others, you are showing that you are empathetic to the struggles of juggling both workplace and outer stressors.
44. **Understand that those you work with have lives outside of the office and that those lives should be the workers' priorities:** This may be one of the most important keys to remember to strengthen relationship management: Ultimately, people's loyalty will default to their families first and foremost, and if you can remember that, you will quickly become a close 2nd in their list of loyalty.
45. **Inspire others to try to succeed, even when the odds are stacked against them:** Be the reason that people try things that

they will most likely fail. Encourage them to try and inspire them by trying to achieve the nearly impossible yourself as well.

46. **Seek to persuade other people without manipulation:** Learn how to ask and receive what you want or need without having to rely on manipulation to get it. If you develop a good enough rapport with those around you, this should be a no-brainer.

47. **Create a productive work environment for yourself and others:** You want to make an environment that people are happy to enter. Happy people are more productive and more loyal people who will be more willing to try to help you if you ask for it.

48. **Always opt for personal interaction as opposed to digital when it is realistic and convenient:** To truly strengthen the bond between yourself and those around you, you should aim to make your communication as personal as possible. If you can do it face-to-face, that is preferred to digital or texting.

49. **Lead by being actively involved in the work rather than by dictating what other people do:** The easiest way to inspire others is to be involved yourself. If they see you in the trenches, they see a leader who is not afraid to help them and get dirty, who is far more trustworthy than a leader who would rather sit back and order people around.

50. **Remember to use your self-awareness, self-management, and social awareness skills in all of your interactions!** As mentioned before, remember that all of your other emotional intelligence skills should be used toward strengthening your relationship management! Do not forget to utilize the most important skills within those quadrants.

12

Conclusion

Hopefully, the information contained in these pages has been beneficial to your understanding of how emotional intelligence works, as well as toward your own current EQ. Throughout this part, you were provided with the knowledge you would need to begin taking control of your EQ and becoming a more emotionally intelligent individual, something that could have lifelong positive benefits to you.

As you make your way through your journey to higher emotional intelligence, be sure to remember some of the key features: You must understand how the four domains of emotional intelligence play off of each other and how each domain is important for social interaction. If you want to be a well-rounded individual, capable of empathy and emotional intelligence, you must have a fundamental understanding and control of your own emotions, as well as the empathy necessary to see how your actions and emotions impact other people. Without that fundamental understanding, your empathy will be meaningless, as you will be unable to relate to those around you.

Remember, you are not trapped at your current emotional intelligence level. Your EQ can grow or shrink based on your own personal behaviors, choices, and development. You can become as charismatic as some of the greatest leaders if you care to put in the effort, or you can retreat as much as you would like and avoid interacting with others. Ultimately, the choice is yours, but research has found that those with higher emotional intelligence levels tend to be happier and healthier.

If you do decide to move forward with bettering your EQ, do not forget the tips provided within these pages! Each tip and challenge requires you to work toward bettering each EQ domain, and if you are able to accomplish all of the challenges and suggestions, you will find your social skills increasing immensely.

Now that you have reached the end of this practical guide, it is time for you to begin! Go out and put your newfound skills to good use in the real world and see where they will take you! Work on strengthening your emotional weaknesses while relying on your strengths that were identified during the assessment. With your newfound knowledge, you are armed with what you will need to begin the process. Good luck, and please feel free to come back to this part as much as is necessary or beneficial to you!

TWO

Emotional Intelligence for Kids

13

Introduction

Nearly every parent has been there. Walking through the grocery store with your child who has been on perfect behavior, everything seems perfectly fine. You are thrilled with your child's good behavior. Then *it* appears. You know what it is.

The dreaded candy aisle.

The child sees the aisle filled with brightly colored candy and asks for a piece, as children tend to do. You tell your child no, that is not a healthy choice, but you are more than happy to allow the child to pick out a piece of fruit or a healthy snack of some sort. You can see it in your child's face; a switch was flipped, and the tantrum is coming.

Suddenly, your child is screaming and flailing in the middle of the candy aisle begging for candy, and you can feel the humiliation burning as brightly as your cheeks. What do you do next?

Some parents may respond with their own emotions, snapping at the child to knock it off, or there will be punishments. Threats to spank, return other food, leave, ground, or otherwise punish the child are voiced, but those only serve to further enrage the child, who may or may not be flailing on the ground and shrieking about you being the worst parent in the world at this point. Emotions continue to rise, and neither side seems willing to listen, and the entire situation escalates.

Other parents prefer to face their children's tantrums with an entirely different tactic altogether. They prefer to teach their children to be emotionally intelligent, and instead, try to solve conflicts with emotion coaching. Through the art of emotion coaching, parents guide their children through five steps: They are aware of their children's emotions, acknowledge emotions as learning opportunities, listen and validate their children's feelings, label emotions, and offer advice on problem-solving. Through these five steps, parents teach children to handle their emotions, good and bad, rather than punishing them for having them. This parent will see the disappointment and frustration in the child and put names to them. Calmly justifying the child's emotions, the emotionally intelligent parent will acknowledge the feelings, saying that he or she can see that the child is very upset and disappointed, as well as relating it to a time that the parent was also disappointed by not getting something desired. The parent would listen as the child confirms that yes, he or she does feel disappointed and upset, and would then offer up a solution to the problem, suggesting that they pick out something healthier but still yummy. Quickly, the tantrum has settled, and the child has learned to identify another feeling and has seen the parent settle the conflict quickly and calmly without letting emotions rule the scenario.

This part teaches you how to approach your children's large feelings from the standpoint of understanding that children cannot inherently control themselves. It recognizes that children, especially younger children, are easily swayed by their emotions and acknowledges that the best way to handle tantrums, anger, frustration, and other negative emotions or behaviors, is to teach children how to think about things in an emotionally intelligent way. This includes being able to identify their own emotions, control their own emotions, and recognize the ways their emotions can impact other people.

Through this part, you will learn the ins and outs of parenting in an emotionally intelligent way and given a step-by-step guide to begin emotion coaching. You will learn the importance of raising a child with a high emotional intelligence quotient (EQ), and you will see just how vastly different your child's behaviors could become if you teach him or her how to act in emotionally intelligent ways. These are lifelong skills that will provide your children with the best chances of success in their futures. Delve into this part now to learn all you need to know about raising emotionally intelligent children.

How is emotional intelligence developed

With an understanding of what emotional intelligence is, you may be wondering how it is developed over time. It all starts in early childhood. The development of EQ begins with the earliest interactions with your child and continues throughout life, constantly changing as you grow and develop as a person. Ultimately, it can also be strengthened and developed like a muscle, rather than being a fixed value.

Natural Development of EQ

Throughout your life, your EQ is being impacted. It is developing as you grow and your brain develops, and ultimately, the EQ you develop by the time you finish adolescence becomes the habitual EQ you utilize throughout adulthood, where it is more or less stable unless you make conscious efforts to alter your behavior. In each of the stages of development, the early years, childhood, adolescence, and adulthood, more is modeled and learned.

The Early Years
Developing EQ begins when the baby is fresh out of the womb. In the earliest days, starting in infancy, your talk of emotions to your child helps him grasp the concepts of what he is feeling and enables him to put a name to them. Your attention to your child when your child is in need models empathy, teaching him to consider other people's needs.

Nurturing your child in the early days, and ensuring that your child has an environment that is secure and consistent is crucial to creating that foundation for emotional intelligence.

The first year of a child's life involves learning self-soothing. Children begin recognizing that they have emotions as they approach one year old, and they begin experimenting with those emotions and how they communicate, such as fake crying to get attention.

Between ages 1 and 2.5, children become more self-aware in general. They recognize that they have emotional responses. Children in this age range are happy and proud when praised, or seem guilty when shamed or feeling as though they have disappointed their parents. They are beginning to learn the words associated with emotions, and begin to show signs of developing empathy, as noted through mimicking faces, or seeming concerned when someone else is crying.

During the preschool years, ages 2-5, children begin to attempt to regulate their emotions, beginning their journey into developing self-management. They may cover their eyes or ears in the response of a stimulus they do not want to see, and they begin to communicate their emotional states more regularly, paying attention to the feelings of others as well. They also begin to develop pretend-play, toying with how emotions and words can have an impact on other people, and they begin to show sympathetic behavior. A child with a sandwich may share half with a child without any food or will offer a hug and a kind word to a peer that is upset, showing the beginnings of developing social awareness and relationship management.

Childhood

Within early elementary school, ranging from ages 5-7, children become more motivated to regulate emotions they would consider self-conscious, such as embarrassment. They are beginning to work on developing problem-solving and coping mechanisms, though they still frequently turn to their parents for help. They are interested in being seen as calm or in control around their peers and work hard to avoid crying or showing other strong displays of anger, sadness, or fear. They are also beginning to get better at investing in other peoples' emotions more and practice further relationship management and social awareness.

Middle childhood, ranging from ages 7-10, marks the time when children begin distancing themselves. They avoid things they dislike or that are troubling, while still working on coping with strong emotions and developing problem-solving skills that will be necessary for relationship management. At this age, children will begin to try to manage relationships, such as smiling at a friend while voicing disapproval or something that they are upset about in order to make sure their friend does not think they no longer like them. They also begin to recognize that they can feel more than one emotion at a time, especially in context with other people, such as being happy to see a friend, but annoyed that the friend did something that bothered him, and they seek to use information they know about other people to help in developing friendships or relationships, furthering social awareness and relationship management skills.

Preadolescence, ranging from ages 10-13, involves a large shift in emotional awareness. They begin to see the world more realistic than the naïve innocent eyes of a young child, and they use their understanding of the world to aid in coping with stress or conflict. They are typically able to develop multiple solutions to problems, which encourages flexibility. They also begin to understand the difference between expressing themselves genuinely with their friends and how they manage their emotions around other people. They may approach their friend to vent their anger and frustration, but to those around them, they may appear as though nothing is wrong. They are able to recognize social roles, such as recognizing various interpersonal relationships, and they begin to develop an idea of how those roles work, which is another crucial aspect of relationship management.

Adolescence

In adolescence, ranging from 13 to adulthood, children become much more aware of the cyclical nature of their emotions. They see how they may feel angry with a friend, but then later feel guilty about feeling angry, and that sort of insight is a motivator to managing relationships and problem-solving tactfully. Teens also begin to understand their own personal values and put more of an importance on them, especially when dealing with stress. People with an emphasis on loyalty may be willing to tolerate more from a friend than someone else, whereas someone who genuinely wants to see the best in people may be quick to forgive, but not forget. Teens also begin to master the art of presenting themselves in ways that are beneficial to them, furthering their self-management skill. They also recognize the mutual nature of relationships. They see how communication has an impact on both people, and effective communication of emotions is crucial to strengthen and maintain good relationships with their friends. They see how their own emotions can hurt their friends, and seek to manage their impact on those around them. By the end of adulthood, all four of the key EQ skills have been developed at about the level they will remain in adulthood without proper intervention.

Strengthening EQ

At any point, EQ can be strengthened. You can strengthen the EQ of your children with age-appropriate methods, or you can strengthen your own through a series of challenges and life changes meant to habituate the behaviors that come together to create your EQ. These six simple practices can help in developing EQ in people that feel the need to further their own development.

Practice identifying all emotions and their accompanying sensations

Self-awareness is the basis of emotional intelligence, and you cannot have highly developed self-awareness if you are unable to identify your emotions. If you find that you struggle to identify your emotions, you should practice doing so. Elevate yourself beyond feeling good or bad—instead, seek to use the most vivid words you can think of. It may be helpful to locate a feelings chart that authors commonly use to elevate their own writing. If you are feeling bad, try to put a more specific name to it. Are you angry? Scared? Sad? If you are angry, is it frustration? Irritation? Jealous? Likewise, if you are feeling good, is it happiness? Contentment? Are you feeling excited? If you make your emotions as specific as possible, you will begin to develop your capacity for identifying them as they are felt in real-time.

Along with naming your emotions you feel, you should make it a point to identify every sensation in your body as it occurs. Feel the quickening of your pulse along with the flash of adrenaline running cold in your veins when you are scared and put a name to the feeling. If you feel the rage burning in your gut, paired with tenseness and a quickened heart rate, name that for what it is. If you are shaking uncontrollably while sobbing, name that feeling. By putting names to the physical sensations as well, you are doubly solidifying your ability to be able to identify and understand your own emotions. This is a good first step! You are well on your way to being able to manage your emotions once you are able to recognize them.

Manage negative emotions

It is easy to get carried away by emotions in general, though the negative ones seem to be far more powerful at swaying our behavior. By learning to manage your emotions, you no longer allow them to have that sway over you. While this is much easier said than done, you will feel far better if you keep those negative emotions from ruling over your reactions.

One of the easiest ways to manage negative emotions is to create a pause between your feelings and behaviors. Whether you take a deep breath or take a few seconds to count to four, you need to create that gap. By creating a delay between emotion and behavior, you are able to let the most intense moment of emotion pass, allowing you to better regulate your behaviors. If your child refuses to do something you have asked, for example, and you immediately feel the anger building up within you, stop, force yourself to take a deep breath, hold it as you count to four, and then exhale and act in a way that is productive instead of a way that will only serve to further exacerbate the situation. Over time, this concept of pausing before acting becomes a habit, enabling you to further control your emotions as you develop self-management.

Choose your words carefully

Vocabulary is everything when communicating with other people. People who have higher EQs typically are able to communicate more efficiently than those who have lower EQs. They are able to choose words in ways that can aid in preventing and correcting miscommunications, and that allows for more immediate action toward conflicts. Word choice is the most basic building block of verbal communication, and if you cannot communicate effectively or tactfully, you are going to struggle in relationships with other people. Whenever you have an interaction that does not quite go the way you were hoping it would take a moment afterward to reflect on the interaction and identify ways you could have communicated better or more clearly. You may be surprised to see that even just tweaking your wording can change the entire mood of the interaction, especially in the context of conflict resolution.

For example, think of how you would react if someone came up to you and shouted, "Wow, why are you so stupid?! You couldn't even clean up that smoothie you spilled on the counter! It's all dried on now! I can't believe you did that; look at the giant mess I'm going to have to clean up because of your carelessness!" Compare that reaction to the one you would have if someone calmly approached you and said, "Hey, I feel really disrespected when you don't clean up after yourself. It makes me feel like my own time is not valued, especially when it takes me so long to clean up after it has sat for a while. Can you please be more mindful of your messes and ensure you clean them up as soon as they happen?"

Look at the key differences in these interactions—one is all about the angry individual blaming you while the other focuses on the individual's own feelings. The one who yelled would likely immediately put you on the defensive, as you suddenly feel attacked and challenged. On the other hand, the calmer response focused on how your actions impacted the other person and how it made them feel, along with a simple request to ensure that it does not happen again. While still awkward to be directly challenged, you are not being attacked in any way. The exchange is quiet, factual, and directed toward the other individual instead of toward you, meaning you do not feel the desperate need to defend yourself.

Now, imagine if you took that concept and projected it elsewhere. You would be focusing on positive language, carefully choosing your words to get the results you would like without conflict. Think about how much happier you and those around you would be if you could solve the conflict by communicating efficiently. You would be able to immediately defuse difficult situations without them blowing up in everyone's faces, and that skill alone is invaluable.

Practice empathetic responses

Empathy is the ability to feel and understand the emotions of those around you. When you empathize with someone, you feel their emotions so deeply and profoundly that it is as if you, yourself, are going through the same situation. It is your ability to intimately relate to another's experiences and provides the feedback necessary to have seamless nonverbal communication of emotions. By being able to look at someone and feel what they are feeling due to being able to relate to them, you will be able to help meet their needs and take care of them. This is also an important cue to let you know when you are overstepping or doing something that is harmful or upsetting to the other person, allowing you to identify that you should take a step back and lighten up on the situation at hand.

You can practice empathy by identifying the feelings of those around you and also imagining yourself in their shoes. If you have a coworker you have been working with who has suddenly become quite difficult to be around, you may ask yourself what is happening in her life to cause so many issues as of late, and you may realize that your coworker's dog had to be put to sleep not too long ago. Imagining what would happen if you had to put your beloved pet down allows you to see further into your coworker's position, and you begin to feel what your coworker is feeling. You understand how deeply having your dog put down would impact you, and you begin to understand why your coworker is short-tempered. Acknowledging the situation enables you to calmly and rationally respond compassionately to the situation. You may be a bit more patient with her, understanding to a degree what she is going through.

Know your triggers

Emotional triggers are the things that have a tendency to set us off. Typically, these stimuli are related to something upsetting and sometimes are connected to something reminiscent of a traumatic event. Whatever the trigger may be, they are often followed by intense, disproportionate responses to stimuli that are considered unwarranted. Someone who is easily triggered by feeling criticized may scream and yell when someone voices that he did something wrong while kindly suggesting a way to fix the mistake. The person who has been triggered is unable to control his reaction and lashes out in his emotional volatility.

Learning to identify your triggers will allow you to recognize when you may be facing an outburst soon, or allow you to avoid the situation altogether. If you know that being criticized is an emotional trigger for you, you can take steps to keep yourself calm when you know that criticism is coming, such as when you go into an annual review for work. Likewise, in parenting, if you know that your toddler screeching the word "NO!" at you tend to send your blood pressure spiking, and you know that it is a common trigger for you, you are able to recognize what is happening once you have identified the word or defiance as your trigger. When you are aware that it is occurring, you are better able to keep it in check, reminding yourself that exploding will not be conducive to parenting and will not better the situation.

Do not give in to adversity

Remember, everyone faces challenges or adversity at some point. It can be tough to deal with these challenges, but despite that, you should persevere. Your reactions to these challenges are a valuable learning experience, even if you react poorly. Remember that even when you make a mistake, or you fall victim to your emotional triggers, or you blow up a conflict, you can fix that mistake. Do not complain and allow yourself to become a victim; instead, look at ways you can learn to avoid that mistake in the future.

After making a mistake, ask yourself questions about what happened to further understand the situation. Keep yourself thinking positively, reminding yourself that every experience has value, no matter how poorly it went, and you are able to set yourself up for success in the future. Remember that failure is not permanent. You can continue to build upon it to strive toward success.

Consider if your child screaming no has triggered your own negative emotions, and in the heat of the moment, you yelled at your child to listen to you. Immediately after yelling, you see the look of panic in your child, followed by your child running away and crying hysterically. Overall, this situation seems like a giant failure, but keep in mind that you can take away knowledge from anything. Remind yourself that you messed up, but it can be turned into a learning experience, for both you and your child. You can go and apologize to your child, telling her that sometimes, even mommy or daddy does something they regret in anger, but it is not okay, and it is important to apologize after hurting someone. You also now have that image of your child afraid of you at that moment to remind you to keep your temper in the future.

15

Raising emotionally intelligent children

Emotional intelligence is important in all aspects of life, and while children do develop some degree of EQ on their own, frequently, the biggest influencers of their EQ is their parents. They learn the foundations for emotional intelligence from their parents, while the rest is formulated by interactions with their peers. Children and teens with higher EQs are typically happier and well-adjusted than their lower EQ peers. They are more skilled at handling intricate social situations and solving conflict without escalating it, and they are typically much better at handling and maintaining their friendships.

Raising an Emotionally Intelligent Child

In the context of this section, the child will refer to any minor child from infancy to preadolescence, differentiating them from teenagers, or adolescence. This age range is where the vast majority of the foundations of emotional intelligence are developed, and they are among the most crucial ages. It is important to understand what you can do in order to help your child develop a healthy amount of emotional intelligence.

How to Encourage Emotional Intelligence in a Child

- **Smile often:** You should smile at your child regularly. This is the beginning of teaching your child to read body language, and also acts to teach empathy.
- **Nurture your child:** By tending to your child's needs, you are teaching your child to put others' needs in front of his or her own, especially when the other person cannot take care of their needs on their own. Your child learns that you are supportive and that you can be trusted. These are behaviors he will seek to emulate later in life.
- **Explain why you say no:** Offer age-appropriate explanations when correcting behavior, with an emphasis on how your child's behavior impacts others. While your child is still quite young and unable to fully comprehend what you are saying, it builds a foundation. The lessons are beginning to be learned, and the vocabulary necessary to be emotionally intelligent is being developed. For example, if your toddler hits you, very gently but firmly tell your child, "No, we do not hit other people. It hurts and makes them sad. Hands are for hugs or high fives instead." In that short dialogue, you set a boundary, explained the reason for the boundary, explained how your child's behavior would hurt other people, and offered an acceptable alternative to the behavior.
- **Listen closely and carefully:** Your child should always feel like communication is open between the two of you. You need to be able to listen and really hear your child when your child approaches you, no matter what the subject is. This teaches the importance of efficient communication, and your child will need those skills in adulthood.
- **Name feelings as they arise:** Starting at an early age, name specific feelings as they are felt. This teaches your child to identify the feelings as language is developing, especially in infancy and the

early toddler years. This foundation is one of the most important building blocks for raising an emotionally intelligent child.

- **Work on problem-solving:** When your child feels stuck on something, instead of swooping in to help, try guiding your child through what she may think she needs to do to solve her problem herself. Ask questions that will point her in the right direction while leaving her free to identify the solution on her own without your input.

- **Model empathy:** Remember, your child is not likely to develop much empathy if your child is never shown empathy. By guiding your child through the steps of empathy and always approaching situations involving your child empathetically, you teach your child to consider emotional states of others as well. Your child will watch you acknowledging his or her feelings and emulate that behavior with others.

- **Model coping with negative feelings:** It is also important to model negative feelings for your child as well. If you are sad and crying in front of your child, that is okay! Turn it into a learning experience and explain that people cry when they are sad. If you are angry, take a deep breath and calm yourself down before explaining that you are angry and why you feel that way. By modeling these negative emotions, you are showing your child that even strong; negative emotions can be managed and worked through. This is a lesson your child will learn and internalize, and it will serve him well

Signs Your Child Needs Extra Support Learning Emotional Intelligence

- **Your child is easily frustrated:** Children struggling with emotional intelligence typically are easily frustrated. If your child seems to blow up at the slightest provocation, such as not having her sandwich sliced just right for lunch, or screaming because you accidentally bumped into her, she may be struggling with emotional regulation.

- **Your child frequently gives up when confronted with a problem:** Oftentimes, children who cannot self-manage feel frustrated when a problem arises. They do not have the flexibility to think about the problem and figure out the best way to solve it, and instead, they give up. They see no reason to try when they are sure they will fail anyway, even though, learning is done in part through failing to succeed.
- **Your child is prone to yelling:** If your child often resorts to yelling when angered or upset, he may be showing signs of low emotional intelligence. Children who yell often do so because they cannot think of how to properly communicate with others, and it seems to be the only option for them to be heard.
- **Your child thinks and speaks negatively:** Children with low EQs are typically hyper-focused on the negative. They may dejectedly talk about how the Lego set they struggled with is stupid, or that they don't like pizza anyway when told they cannot have it for dinner. Instead of being able to cope with their negative feelings, they instead allow the negativity to color everything.
- **Your child struggles to ask for help:** Children struggling with EQ often do not ask for help, or when they do, they do not do it in the best way they could. They struggle with communication, and because of that, they cannot quite clearly convey that they need extra help or support, whether emotional or with schoolwork or chores.
- **Your child struggles to make friends and maintain relationships:** Children who struggle with emotional intelligence typically also struggle to maintain relationships with other children. If you notice that your child is struggling to make friends, or is frequently cast aside by others, especially if there are other signs

of low emotional intelligence present as well, your child may need extra help and support navigating social situations.

Raising an Emotionally Intelligent Teen

Teens are a little tougher to influence than children just due to the nature of adolescence. Teens are seeking to put as much distance between themselves and their parents as possible as they prepare to leave the nest and make their debuts into adulthood. Their bodies are going through an intense hormonal shift from a child into adults capable of reproduction, and those hormones create intense feelings that can be difficult to navigate. Further, teens also feel the pull of peer pressure and self-consciousness as they struggle to find their places in society. With a few tips in mind, you can help encourage emotional intelligence before your child leaves the nest for good. Remember, all of the tips for raising emotionally intelligent children also apply to teens.

How to Encourage Emotional Intelligence in a Teen

- **Ask Guiding Questions:** Remember, teens are all about rebellion and doing the exact opposite of what their parents say. Teens want to do things their own way, and that is okay! It is a normal part of growing up and separating from parents. This means, however, that you cannot just tell the teen how to do something, especially when it comes to conflicts or relationships with those around her. Instead, try to ask guiding questions to gently lead the teen to the answer on her own. If your child is upset about an interaction with a friend, you can try asking, "What would you feel if your friend treated you like that?" or "What would you like the other person to do if roles were reversed?" Sometimes, teens are thinking about things in a self-centered manner and need that little extra push to start thinking about how other people might see how their behavior. Teens, by and large, do not want to feel embarrassed or self-conscious at all, and once you have them thinking about how they would respond to someone else doing the same thing, they may see the error in their ways without needing you to overtly point them out.

- **The "Maybe" Game:** The "Maybe" game involves understanding why others do what they do. If you see someone out and about who is in a bad mood, each person in the family should suggest a potential reason for the bad mood. For example, if you see someone ranting and raving to a manager about how his meal was not quite right and he demands a refund when your family goes out to dinner, have each person take a moment to suggest why he is in such a bad mood. "Maybe he's getting a divorce." "Maybe he just lost someone close to him." "Maybe he just got fired." "Maybe it's his birthday, and he has no one to spend it with." "Maybe he got into a fender bender." This begins to solidify to your teen the habits of trying to understand the context of emotions rather than just seeing the emotions themselves. When you are able to understand the what and the why behind emotions in other people, you are developing empathy skills, and this is a fantastic opportunity for teens. As it is habituated, the teen is more likely to bring those skills to interpersonal conflicts with friends, and instead of being annoyed or angry when a friend is upset or irritable, your teen will be able to stop and start figuring out why emotions are running as high as they are.
- **Praise behavior that shows high emotional intelligence:** Just as with younger children, teens love to be praised. They may act embarrassed about it at the moment, but acknowledging when your child is doing well reinforces the good behavior. If your teen acknowledges your feelings when you confront him about not doing the dishes, you should praise the act of acknowledging your feelings. If your teen solves a conflict with siblings in a constructive manner, praise that. Let your teen know you are watching

and that you see how much effort he is putting into behaving thoughtfully. He will appreciate it.

- **Be empathetic:** Modeling good emotional intelligence does not end when your child hits the teen years. Showing empathy to your teen, and especially with your teen around, teaches her to cue into other people's emotions. If she sees you putting in the effort to understand how other people are really feeling, she will learn that that is an important part of social interactions. If your teen is upset about a breakup, for example, you could make it a point to go to your teen and tell her about the first time you broke up with someone and how much that hurt. Label her feelings, let her know that you can see how upset she is, and show her that you are there for her if she wants to talk, or if what she needs is a pint of ice cream and some movies to binge-watch on her own.
- **Pay attention for signs your teen is struggling:** You know your teen better than anyone, though it may not always feel that way. You should pay attention to behavioral changes or signs that your teen is struggling to cope in an emotionally healthy manner. If you see signs that your teen is struggling, do not try to explain it as a one-time issue, and instead make it a point to address the problem. For example, if you notice that your teen is putting an extra emphasis on social media, obsessing over it and trying to look Instagram ready at all time, you may want to intervene. Putting in all of his energy to one thing can become a problem if unaddressed, and while teens revel in the attention, they may get on social media, putting their entire sense of self-worth on how many likes or shares or followers they get is unhealthy. If your child's teacher approaches you with concerns about behavior as well, it is important that you pay attention and follow up. If your child is struggling in school, where you are not likely to see, your child may need more support than you can offer, and it may be time to consider getting a professional involved.

- **Avoid trivializing your teen's feelings:** As an adult that is removed from most situations within your teen's social life, you can quickly identify when you feel as though your teen is being melodramatic or over-exaggerating a problem. While the solution may be clear-cut to you, remember that it is not necessarily that clear to your teen. Do not disregard your teen's feelings as illegitimate or irrational. Remember, emotions are the opposite of rationality, and they do not have to make sense; they only have to be acknowledged. Make sure that you do not invalidate your teen's feelings. Trivializing your teen's feelings is not empathetic and does not help your teen learn to acknowledge and manage her own feelings. Instead, it teaches her that her emotions should be ignored or disregarded, which only serves to make situations worse. Emotions are important and should be acknowledged and legitimized, no matter how much you, as a third party, can see that they are not necessarily warranted to the extent that they are felt. Struggling to regulate the intensity of emotions is a sign of lower emotional intelligence, and learning to regulate them is a skill that takes practice. That can only be practiced through living through the stronger emotions and learning coping skills that work for the individual.
- **Seek therapy if necessary:** If all else fails, and you feel as though your teen is struggling to cope or develop appropriate levels of emotional intelligence, seeking a professional trained in guiding teens through the process is an acceptable option. Therapy is beneficial to nearly everyone and can teach your child some very important coping mechanisms that will last a lifetime. If this step is necessary for your teen, start by speaking to his primary care physician to get a referral.

Signs Your Teen Needs Extra Support Learning Emotional Intelligence

- **Your teen does not perform well in school:** Teens with lower EQs struggle in school due to their struggles socially. They may withdraw and not put in the effort necessary to be successful, or they may be too afraid to ask for help when they need it, getting overwhelmed easily and instead choosing to give up.
- **Your teen is overly-critical:** If your teen has some sort of harsh criticism of everything, even when it is not constructive, he may struggle with EQ. He may not see how his words impact others, or he may struggle with communicating efficiently in ways that would come across constructively. He also is prone to criticizing everything as a coping mechanism for struggling in the first place.
- **Your teen bullies others:** Teens who have lower EQs frequently have their own frustrations build up, feeling self-conscious and misunderstood. Because they struggle to identify or regulate their own feelings, as well as the struggle to really understand how their actions hurt others, they frequently lash out at other people and may even bully others in order to try to make themselves feel better, or as an impulsive reaction to feeling sensitive or self-conscious.
- **Your teen struggles to control anger:** Teens who have lower EQs tend to struggle with controlling their anger. As having self-management skills is a fundamental component of emotional intelligence, it is a common weakness of those struggling with their EQs.
- **Your teen constantly blames everyone else for problems:** While people with higher EQs tend to control their emotions in order to grant them clarity to see situations rationally and aid in problem-solving, those with lower EQs tend to struggle with that. Someone with lower EQ sees themselves as a victim much of the time, not acknowledging how his or her own negativity or lack

of communication may have contributed to things blowing up. Your teen may struggle to see how he or she is involved in negative situations and instead seeks to push the blame of friendships failing or conflicts exploding on everyone but him or herself.

- **Your teen cannot cope when plans change:** Flexibility typically comes naturally to people with higher EQs. Since they have a better handle on their emotions, they are more able to cope when things go wrong, leading to a much more flexible person in general. When your teen struggles with her EQ, she may be unable to deal with changes in a healthy manner as a result. Your teen may have made plans with friends, and when a friend cancels, or the group decides to do something different, the disappointment and negative emotions may become overwhelming for her.

- **Your teen is negative and pessimistic:** Teens who struggle to self-regulate frequently find themselves stuck in a constant loop of negativity. Their negative feelings breed more negativity, keeping that mindset. Teens with lower EQs tend to look at things pessimistically instead of shifting their mindsets toward positivity, which is typically much more productive.

- **Your teen struggles to read body language:** Emotional intelligence is all about being able to understand other people. People with high EQs are adept at looking at a person and being able to see exactly what they are feeling based on body language alone. If your teen seems to be unable to read the body language of yourself or other people, it may be a sign of struggling with emotional intelligence.

- **Your teen gives up easily:** People who struggle with emotional intelligence frequently prefer to give up rather than keep trying when they face adversity. They feel as though they cannot cope with the negative feelings that come along with struggling, and instead prefer to give up. Giving up and playing the victim role is easier than struggling to proceed, even if giving up eliminates all chances of success. Your teen may struggle with a question on a homework assignment, and instead of persevering and trying to work past it, he instead decides not to do any of it, even though he likely would have still gotten a good grade on it, even missing the one question.

- **Your teen is more confrontational and argumentative than normal:** Teens who struggle with emotional intelligence typically fall victim to arguing. Even if the other person has disengaged, the teen with a lower EQ is likely to keep pushing the point. They cannot accept the possibility of them not being right, no matter how much the other person tells them they are done discussing this. If your teen feels like she has to win every argument, she gets into, no matter how inane, or how wrong she was, she may need to work on her EQ.

16

Parenting styles in regards to Emotional Intelligence

Everyone parents differently. There are various different parenting styles for a wide range of situations, and those parenting styles can yield vastly different results. Every parent is going to have their own methods, but unfortunately, some are not as beneficial to children as others. Certain parenting styles are absolutely more conducive to raising healthy children. The four types of parents in terms of acknowledging and handling children's emotions are dismissing, disapproving, laissez-faire, and emotion coaching. Each of these types of parenting creates different types of children, and of the four, emotion coaching parents are the most likely to create happy, well-adjusted, emotionally intelligent children.

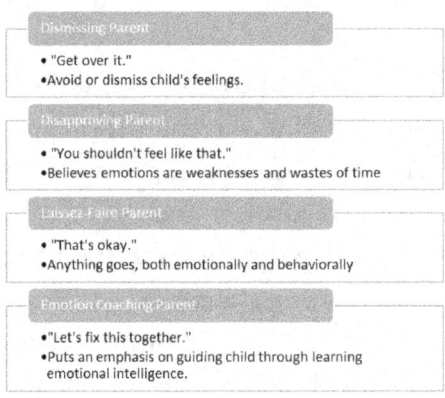

The Dismissing Parent

Dismissing parents are typically prone to avoiding or dismissing their children's emotions whenever possible. They seek to stop emotions and distract from them, as opposed to recognizing that they should be worked through. Dismissing parents typically tell their children to get over it when they are faced with tough emotions, implying that the child's feelings are unimportant. They would soon ignore the emotions than help fix the problem. They see emotions as troublesome, instead of as an opportunity to connect with and support their children, and will oftentimes downplay the event leading to emotion as not being that bad.

Typically, the dismissing parent will say things like telling the child that there is no reason to be angry, sad, afraid, or whatever else she is feeling. The problem with this is that the child learns that emotions are not to be trusted, and may even lead to the child being unable to trust her own gut reactions. If the child grew up being told not to feel certain ways or that she has no reason to feel the way she does, she is likely to believe that her own feelings are untrustworthy and irrelevant. From a perspective of developing emotional intelligence, it is easy to see how feeling as though you cannot trust your own emotions would lead for you to struggle to accurately identify what you are feeling at any given time. This can have major negative repercussions on a child's emotional health.

Further, dismissing parents also typically dismiss their own emotions as well, while also discouraging the child from speaking emotionally with her parents. The dismissing parent may be uncomfortable with emotions in general, or may just not understand how to work through emotions. They see the passage of time as the perfect cure as opposed to developing real problem-solving abilities.

The dismissing parent results in a child who believes there is something inherently wrong with her. She feels inadequate, and as though her perception of reality is skewed if she is feeling inappropriate ways.

She learns to dismiss her own emotions rather than seeing them as important. She does not see the benefit in attempting to talk about her emotions, as they have always been considered irrelevant or inaccurate. She is also likely to learn that problem solving is not necessary, as she believes that time will resolve any issues she encounters.

Consider a child who is feeling quite angry at that particular moment. You, a dismissive parent, see your child melting down, screaming because he really wanted that new toy at the store. Instead of talking your child through it, you tell your son, "Oh, come on. It's not that bad. You'll get over it. There's no reason to be that mad over this; you have three other toys at home that are really similar to this one. What's the problem?" This, of course, does nothing to help the child actually get over it. Just because it was suggested does not mean it will happen, and just because you may not see being denied the toy as a big deal, your child certainly did.

The Disapproving Parent

The disapproving parent, like the dismissing parent, sees emotions as inconvenient or a problem that needs to be avoided at all costs. The disapproving parent, instead of saying that the feelings should be gotten over, says that the child should not feel the way he or she does, to begin with. Emotions are seen as a sign of weakness, and expressing them is seen as even worse. They disregard their own emotions while also encouraging their children to do the same, treating any emotions a child may express negatively. One of the most commonly heard phrases from the disapproving parent is, "You should not feel like that!" and is typically followed with threats if the child does not get his act together and stop the show of emotions.

Typically, the disapproving parent believes that emotions, particularly negative ones, are a waste of time. There is no point in wasting time or energy focusing on emotions when they are unimportant anyway, and for that reason, they are typically disregarded, or even punished.

They also sometimes feel as though children use negative emotions as a manipulation tactic rather than seeing them as legitimate. Because of the perceived manipulative nature of the emotions felt, the disapproving parent sees emotions as something that needs to be quashed rather than encouraged or taught to control.

Typically, the disapproving parent is far more negative and judgmental of emotions and is typically authoritative. They are far harsher than the dismissive parent and seek to control and criticize all expressions of emotion. The repercussions of this are quite similar to what happened as a result of dismissing parents: Children grow up out of touch with their emotions. They learn to dismiss and ignore their emotions rather than learning to control or cope with them. They never learn how to properly name their emotions, and they certainly never learn good ways to deal with other people's emotions, typically defaulting to dismissing or disapproving of them.

Let's again revisit the child who felt angry about not getting the toy at the store. If you were a disapproving parent, you likely would have told your child, "Stop overreacting! You shouldn't feel like this over a toy! It's just a chunk of plastic. Stop your whining and stop acting like a crybaby, or I'll treat you like one. If you don't stop your whining right now, you will regret it. I'll take one of your toys at home and throw it away!" Instead of coaching your child through feeling emotions, you command and threaten to make the emotion disappear, though this is rarely effective. If the child does obey, it is out of fear of the consequences more so than out of being able to control emotions in a healthy manner. Despite the disapproving parent's stance on the matter, a child's emotions do not make him weak, nor does a child need to forego emotions in order to survive. In fact, it is quite the opposite: Children need to learn to manage their emotions in order to survive in a social setting. A child will never learn to interact in meaningful, emotionally intelligent manners if he is never granted the ability to explore emotions in a safe setting without worrying about threats or punishments.

The Laissez-Faire Parent

Laissez-faire is derived from French, literally translating to "let it be." Parents who are deemed laissez-faire are typically permissive, to a fault. They allow all emotions to be felt and treat all emotions as acceptable, with no regard for the behavior that may follow them. The children are free to feel. However, they feel and are never taught the ways necessary to mitigate the control emotions may have over them.

This sort of permissive attitude means they are never able to develop important coping mechanisms that allow for them. These children are raised without structure or support they need, and while it is important to allow children to feel their emotions in order to develop thorough self-awareness, the children also need the guidance to help them through handling those emotions. The skill to handle those emotions is not learned solely through experiencing the emotions. They need to be taught coping methods and problem-solving skills that the laissez-faire parent disregards. Rather than teaching children to cope, the laissez-faire parent allows for the feelings to be felt until they run their course, much like how the dismissing parent considered the time the ultimate coping mechanism.

Unfortunately, this sort of permissive parenting brings a whole new slew of problems to the child. Children raised by laissez-faire parents typically struggle with self-control. They are typically quite disobedient and impulsive, while still being quite dependent at the same time. Because they were never encouraged to develop much past the early childhood ages emotionally and they never felt many consequences for their actions from their parents, they never developed the skills they would need to problem solve on their own. These children typically struggle to self-regulate or self-soothe when feeling intense negative emotions, and also likely struggle to make friends since they never learned to pick up on social cues necessary for social success. Most children do not want to play with the kid who does not realize how his own behaviors impact others.

Again, we will revisit the example of the child complaining at the store because he was not allowed to buy a toy. As a laissez-faire parent, you would look at your child throwing a tantrum for a moment, nod your head, and say, "Okay," while continuing to go about your business, offering no support for your child. You would not be discouraging the emotional expression, but you would also not be teaching your child to express himself. This teaches your child that emotions are acceptable, but also teaches your child that his tantrum is an acceptable way to deal with them. Since you did not correct the behavior, the child believes it is acceptable by default. In those early days where you are setting the stage, you never teach your child that sort of behavior is unacceptable, and those behaviors are repeated elsewhere, where people are far less tolerant. This, of course, then makes your child typically avoided or disliked, as he is incapable of dealing with his emotions appropriately and becomes an annoyance to those around him.

The Emotion Coaching Parent

The last of the four styles of parenting is emotion coaching. This style of parenting puts an emphasis on practicing empathy and guiding the child through emotions. The emotion coaching parent seeks to teach the child how to identify his emotions and how those emotions affect him, as well as those around him. These parents value teaching and guiding rather than allowing the child to learn through trial and error. They seek to be involved, but not controlling of their children, and that balance enables them to be effective with their parenting approach.

Emotion coaching parents do value all emotions and teach their children that all emotions are important and acceptable to feel, but not all behaviors, especially those that are emotionally motivated, are acceptable. Behaviors that are harmful or not productive are typically discouraged, with the parent gently guiding the child through processes to better cope with the feelings and emphasize thinking critically to solve problems effectively. Through patience, empathy, and time, emotion coaching parents are able to create emotionally intelligent young children who develop higher EQs.

Children raised by emotion coaching parents are usually much more well-adjusted than children who were not. They typically do better in social settings, making friends more often, and maintaining those relationships better. They are usually able to control and regulate their own feelings and reactions, no matter how angry or upset they may be. They are much better at self-soothing, allowing them to regulate their behaviors and keep from doing things they will regret later due to impulse control issues. They are usually happier because their emotions are not a point of contention for them, and they are typically closer to their parents, seeing parents as valuable teachers and reliable support in times of need.

We once again return to the example of the child throwing a tantrum who is crying because he wants a toy you have declined to buy. As an emotion coaching parent, you would get down to his eye level and put a hand on his shoulder. You would calmly voice that he looks angry and disappointed that he is not getting the new toy and that you understand that. You would also remind him that just because he is angry does not mean that he can throw a tantrum in the store, and you would offer an alternative, such as taking a deep breath to calm down so he can use his words to communicate with you. The end result is a child who feels acknowledged, heard, and valued.

17

Marriage, Divorce and your Child's Emotional health

Your child is deeply impacted by every aspect of your romantic relationship with her other parent. If her parents share a happy, healthy relationship, your child learns to expect that. On the other hand, if your child sees an emotionally unhealthy relationship, that becomes what she learns to expect in her future. Your relationship impacts your child's emotional health, whether you want it to or not. No matter how hard you may try to keep some aspects away from your child, she will see it for what it is.

Marriage and Your Child

Especially if your marriage is to the child's other parent, your child will see the two of you as one unit. You and your spouse are the child's natural family unit, and it is a given that the two of you will be together. They will develop an opinion on the nature of your relationship, and that will color their expectations for the future. For this reason, it is incredibly important for you to model a healthy marriage for your child to see. Ask yourself if your relationship with your spouse is one that you would like your child to live in as well, and if not, it may be time to make some serious changes to your relationship.

In a healthy marriage, your child will see you and your spouse modeling empathy, conflict resolution, and genuinely caring for each other. This modeling sets a serious example for your child and should be fostered and encouraged. They should see you and your spouse, both during good and bad times. Conflict is okay, so long as they also see the resolution of the conflict as well. You want to make sure you are modeling those conflict resolution skills and making it clear that marriage and love do not have to be perfect. Conflict is inevitable and does not mean a relationship is doomed. What is important is whether you and your spouse can resolve the conflict, especially with young eyes watching closely to see how you handle the situation.

When you stay in a toxic marriage, your child sees it all. No matter how hard you may try to hide it, your child is absorbing what is going on. Your child will feel helpless and frightened of the tension that hangs in the room whenever both parents are present. They may even begin to internalize that blame on themselves. They may even try to fix the problems they see, essentially becoming the adult in the house, so to speak, as they try to smooth over conflicts, instead of their parents being the ones to guide them through the process of developing healthy coping skills. This essentially forces the child to grow up far too early, which can cause many emotional issues for your child or teen.

Children growing up within a toxic marriage, depending on their personality, either internalize shame and guilt, feeling insecure most of the time and frightened by their parents' interactions, especially when there is plenty of yelling about hate from both sides. Your child, especially at a younger age, identifies closely with both parents, and to hear one parent say they hate the other is something young children internalize and take to mean the parent hates them too. They develop low self-esteem and often feel unworthy of loving themselves, considering they may have internalized the blame for the conflicts and disagreements. They learn to model unhealthy relationships, not knowing any different, and this sets them up for romantic failure later in life. If all they see is yelling to solve arguments, they will likely resort to yelling within their own romantic relationships as well.

If you have read this book this far, you may begin to recognize some of the effects of toxic marriages on children as signs of low EQ. The child is locked in a loop of negativity, accepting helplessness. This is a sign of low self-management. The child may act out regularly around other people, showing low self-awareness. They may struggle in relationships in the future, showing low social awareness and relationship management. Staying in a toxic marriage sets your child up for emotional failure later in life and is something that should be avoided. When the choices are - a child growing up either with parents in a toxic marriage or happily divorced parents, the happily divorced parents will always be the best option, even if it cuts the time the child sees parents in half.

Divorce and Your Child

Sometimes, divorce is the best option within a marriage. Things may have escalated so far that neither spouse is willing or able to reconcile, and one or both partners feel as though they would be better off without the other. This does not necessarily have to mean that one of the parents was a bad person; sometimes, two people do not mesh well and simply bring out the worst in each other. Divorce will always be difficult for your child, but there are ways for you to minimize the damage. Children are resilient, and while they may struggle at first, they will bounce back with the proper support and guidance.

Children, especially at the younger ages, may see divorce as an impossibility or refuse to acknowledge or accept it. It is likely that your marriage is all your child has ever known if you are still married to their other parent, and that sudden dissolution of his family unit can be absolutely devastating. No matter how peaceful your divorce may be, it will have negative effects on your children. The negative effects of the child's parents divorcing can be seen in all aspects of life, especially if the child struggles to cope with the change. Those with a lower EQ are more likely to suffer to a greater extent, though even children with higher EQs are going to struggle to cope to some degree. Oftentimes, children who have gone through a divorce are likely to experience emotional instability, they may out, experience depression or anxiety, or struggle in school.

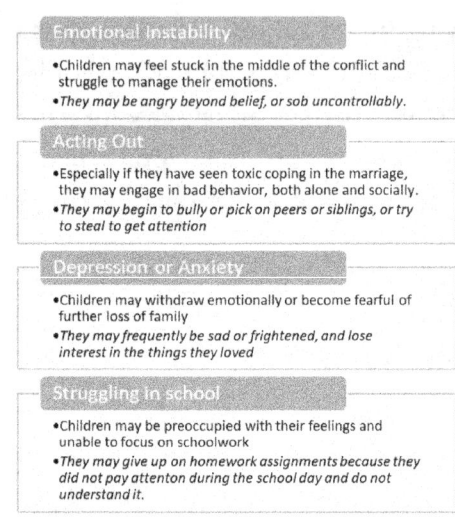

Children with lower EQs will need much more guidance in coping with divorce than children with higher EQs, but they will be able to do so, given the right support. Understanding the ins and outs of emotion coaching will be essential in aiding your child to cope with the loss of a family unit, he may never have been able to even imagine would degrade. Remember to acknowledge your child's feelings to help him cope with such sudden changes, and to keep in mind that it may take your child some serious time to begin to comprehend such drastic changes. Further, children with lower EQs may struggle to ask for the support they need from you as they need it.

Children with higher EQs are likely to cope with their feelings better in general. They typically are better at handling their emotions, and while they may be devastated at such a drastic change, they can typically manage their reactions better. You still may face them acting out as they struggle, but you can typically speak with them and help them work through it. They are able to communicate their own feelings with you better, which enables you to give them the support that they need and ask for. Your child with a higher EQ is also likely to be more resilient in general than a child with a lower EQ. She will have the coping skills that will be beneficial for coming to terms with the divorce. While your child with higher EQ will still struggle in similar ways to the child with a lower EQ, overall, your child will be better equipped to cope.

Divorce and Your Teen

Teenagers, despite their increased levels of maturity, are still inclined to struggle when their world is rocked in such a drastic manner. Like children, teens have come to identify their family unit and having that suddenly and irrevocably destroyed can be absolutely devastating. They have always known things to be a certain way, and maybe reluctant to see how things will change and evolve. Teens are likely to go through a stage of denial, in which they refuse to acknowledge the impending changes. While they may try to pretend to be mature about things, they are still likely to be deeply hurt at the idea of losing their family and will act out accordingly.

Like children, they tend to show similar signs of emotional distress. They may suddenly regress and become less able to control or regulate their own emotions, even if they were pros at it before. They may become angry or upset, and constantly resort to criticism to lash out at those around them, likely as a result of criticism being present in a degrading marriage. Oftentimes, when marriages fail, there was conflict in the home long before the divorce, and the teen will typically try to act accordingly. They may show signs of negativity. They feel as though their family, who has been the vast majority of their world for most of their lives, is shattering. They struggle to cope with the loss of that family unit.

Teens whose parents are divorcing are also more likely to rebel or act out than their peers, often engaging in antisocial behaviors. They may engage in risky acts, such as unsafe sex or experimenting with drugs and alcohol as a way of trying to cope with the loss of attention and affection from one parent. In a divorce, at least one parent loses out on their parent-child relationship, and more frequently, both parents lose out on it as custody is split. The teen, feeling the need to cope with it somehow, seeks the affection and attention elsewhere, even if their methods for attaining it are rather extreme. These rebellious acts, such as stealing or engaging in unsafe sex, can lead to lifelong consequences, especially if your teen is close to adulthood and gets caught committing crimes, gets an STI, gets pregnant, or impregnates someone else.

Teens whose parents are divorcing, especially if the divorce is particularly messy or painful, are at a higher risk for becoming entangled in addiction or drug abuse as they seek out alternative ways to cope with their painful, overwhelming feelings during such a difficult time. Despite the risks, they engage in these acts anyway if they find it lessens the pain at all. This can have lifelong implications, as not only can addiction ruin a person's life, it could potentially kill them. They may not think about the risks, or rather, they may choose not to care about the risks, and continue to engage anyway if they choose to go down this road.

Like children, teens also may struggle with academic performance in the event of a divorce. Due to the emotional turmoil, they may have been exposed to; they may find it difficult to focus on tasks at hand in school and instead eventually just accept the struggles and failures. Their grades begin to suffer, which can have lifelong implications on the teen, especially if prior to the divorce, she was interested in going to a university.

Emotional Distress
- May be overall negative or show signs of depression or anxiety
- *They may begin to lash out or regress in their ability to manage emotions*

Rebellious Acts
- May engage in risky behavior to rebel as a way to regain control
- *They may experiement with drugs, sex, or criminal behavior*

Risk of Addiction
- May be more likely to engage in risky drug use that leads to addiction or dependency

Struggling with Academics
- May feel unable to focus in school
- *They may begin to fail classes, miss assignments, or even skip school altogether*

As children, teens with higher EQs are a bit more equipped to deal with these situations as they arise. They may be devastated and upset, but they are still more resilient than their peers. They will still require support, but with their improved emotional intelligence skills, they will do far better in the long run. They will not be as impulsive, and while they may be moodier than usual, they are less likely to try to cope by resorting to dangerous and unhealthy habits. They are far more likely to look at the risks and decide they are not worth them and will be more likely to be able to find the good in situations, no matter how bad the situations may be. The higher the teen's EQ, the better they are likely to take the divorce, especially if they feel blindsided by it, to begin with.

18

The Father's crucial role

No one will argue that fathers are not important in a child's development. After all, it takes two parents to make a child, so it makes sense that two parents are optimal for raising a child. As society has changed, the father's role in child-rearing has also changed. Nowadays, fathers are far more involved with parenting than they ever were before, and because of that, their roles in raising children are becoming further studied. Research on emotional intelligence has begun to discover that the father's role is maybe even more important than previously believed.

The Relationship Between Father and Child's Emotional Intelligence

From birth, fathers have an impact on their children. Children who grow up with a father actively involved in their lives are more likely to grow up to be more emotionally secure. They are more confident and willing to explore and take chances. As they age, they develop to have better relationships of all kinds than peers who grew up without a father. Children who grow up with fathers are more likely to perform better in school and less likely to commit crimes. But why?

The answer is emotional intelligence.

Fathers with higher EQs are more interested in being involved with their children's upbringing, and their interactions with their children reflect emotional intelligence. They are more likely to be nurturing, empathetic, and supportive in the way that their children need because of their EQs, and in turn, their children grow up to become emotionally intelligent as well. Because children see their father's EQ modeled for them throughout their early development, they naturally tend to take the skills equivalent to their father's EQ.

A study testing for a relationship between children and fathers' emotional intelligence found that there was, in fact, a statistically significant relationship between a father and his children's emotional intelligence. The study, performed by Mojgan Mirza and Ma'rof Redzuan in Malaysia, found that the majority of children studied that tested with higher EQs had fathers that were also emotionally intelligent. The conclusion found that fathers are statistically significant to the development of their children's emotional intelligence.

This study was conducted studying Iranian students within Iranian primary schools in the city of Kuala Lumpur, Malaysia. They studied 107 father-child pairs, with the children ranging from 8-10 years old, and the fathers being a graduate or Ph.D. students at the universities throughout the country, ranging from ages 25 to over 40. They used the Bar-On EQ-i to test for the father's emotional intelligence while using the EQ-i Youth Version for the children, along with a short questionnaire about demographics. Within every category, the scientists tested (intrapersonal, interpersonal, stress management, adaptability, general mood, and total emotional intelligence), there was a statistically significant relationship. This means that the father's own emotional intelligence was statistically reflected in their children's own EQs.

The Importance of the Father's EQ

If the father has a significant influence over his children's EQ, it should come as no surprise that the father's role in childrearing is important. Fathers play a crucial role in developing cognitive, behavior, and general health. Further, boys who have grown up with a positive male role model tend to develop better, more positive gender-role characteristics. They are more likely to be positive male role models themselves when they grow up. Girls who grow up with positive male role models tend to develop better opinions of men in general, as well as develop a better understanding of men.

Children with involved fathers tend to do better educationally and are associated with stronger communication skills, critical thinking, and academic achievement in adolescents. This may be due to the fact that compared to mothers, fathers spend a larger portion of their one-on-one interactions engaging in play than mothers do. These playful interactions become the basis for children learning to manage their emotions and behaviors.

Overall, the father's contribution to the child's emotional intelligence is just as significant as the mother's. Fathers with higher EQs tend to have some of the following traits:

- Engage emotionally with his children's own emotional states (empathetic)
- Avoids telling children how to feel
- Teaches problem-solving skills
- Guides children through challenges through adversity and everyday challenges
- Positively models management of negative, strong emotions
- Makes time to play with children

Each of those traits has significant impacts on a child's emotional development. The emotionally intelligent father is empathetic, focuses on problem-solving, and models positive coping mechanisms. Because children learn through play, they often emulate their fathers in play. They learn to develop their fathers' behaviors because those are what is modeled. If a father shows signs of low EQ, the children are likely to follow suit.

Effect of Father's EQ for Children in Action

Now that it has been established that fathers are incredibly important to the development of EQ for children, let's take a few moments to see this in action. We will follow two different situations: A child who is afraid of the dark and cries at bedtime, and a teen who refused to do the dishes after dinner and has now lost electronics privileges and throwing a fit about it. We will look at each of these situations and how they would be likely to play out with both low and high EQ fathers, paying attention to both the father's actions and the child or teen's responses.

Low EQ Father Interacting with Child

Ava, a 9-year-old, is terrified of the dark. She always has been, and she struggles to sleep without a night light, or without the hall light on. Every time the light is turned off, Ava cries and begs for it to be turned back on. If it gets turned off before Ava's father heads to bed and Ava wakes up in the middle of the night, she screams in terror and begs for help and for her light to be turned back on. When asked what her problem is, she never has a clear answer, instead just insisting that she is scared.

Her father, assuming he has a lower EQ, hears Ava screaming in her room in the middle of the night. He jumps out of bed, furious about the interruption, and storms to her bedroom, flinging the door open and further terrifying the child. Without stopping to see that his child is scared or in need of comfort, he immediately begins to yell. "What is wrong with you?! Just go to sleep! You shouldn't be afraid of the dark—you aren't a baby! There are no monsters in the dark! Just *stop crying and go to sleep!*"

Of course, this tirade does nothing to help Ava calm down. She hears her father yelling, and suddenly a monster in the dark seems far more real to her. She sees her father's face, but all she hears is the monster that is his rage, roaring at her to stop being afraid. She cries more uncontrollably at the situation, and her father responds in turn by shutting her door and leaving her in the dark to further cry to herself in fear.

He disregards her feelings, downplays and dismisses them, and acts in ways that do not exemplify problem-solving or teaching her to cope with her fear. Instead of helping her, he threw fuel on the fire, and she has learned that he cannot be trusted in critical moments when she is terrified. She learns that yelling at people that are annoying you is acceptable and that children do not need to be comforted or taken care of during periods of emotional turmoil. Her father's low EQ is learned by her as well, and she never is taught the proper way to manage her emotions.

High EQ Father Interacting with Child

Now, imagine Ava's father within this scene with a higher EQ. He hears the sound of his daughter crying out for him in fear. Despite his initial annoyance at being woken up yet again, he takes a deep breath and gets up to tend to his daughter, reminding himself that she is having a hard time and needs the extra support.

He arrives at her room and sees his daughter sobbing in bed. "What's wrong?" he asks. He tries to encourage her to verbalize how she is feeling in hopes of being able to suggest actions to help with the situation. He reaches over to hug his daughter, recognizing that his child needs extra support during this emotional event. She shakes her head no in response, not answering. "Are you scared?" She nods. "Why?" She shrugs.

Seeing that this situation is not likely to be resolved by speaking alone and recognizing that getting frustrated is likely to only escalate the situation further, her father decides to offer solutions instead of fighting to tell her that she is wrong and being irrational. He understands that he cannot control her emotions and that she may be struggling to control them herself.

Instead of arguing, berating Ava, or lashing out angrily, her father instead offers up a few solutions. He asks if she wants her desk lamp on to sleep and she nods her head, tearfully looking up at her father. He obliges and turns it on. While he really only substituted one sleep crutch (sleeping with the hall light on) for another (sleeping with the lamp on), he has proven that he is supportive of his child. He offered her a solution that she accepted, and he is able to go off to sleep after another quick hug and reminding her that she is safe and to let him know if she needs anything else.

In this situation, despite the fact that Ava's father was frustrated, he acted with emotional intelligence. He did not take his frustration out on Ava, despite how much he may have been angry at being woken up yet again. He did not leave Ava to deal with her problem on her own. He did not belittle her feelings or demean her. He acted compassionately and approached the situation, knowing that his own interactions with her would set the stage for future interactions. If she felt as though she could not trust him, she would not be able to express her feelings, now or later. He offered a solution that was acceptable, helping her solve the problem and reminding her that she has the option to sleep with a lamp turned on if she needs it.

In this situation, Ava learned that her father approaches her with empathy and compassion, two skills that she is far more likely to internalize if she is typically on the receiving end of them. She learned to look for solutions for problems instead of staying the victim and being afraid to try to fix the problem. She learned that her emotions are allowed to be expressed and that she can trust her father to help her if she needs his support, no matter how inconvenient it may have been. She begins to pick up her father's higher EQ skills by watching them modeled for her.

Low EQ Father of Teen

Now, let's imagine teenaged Brian. He hates doing chores more than anything and constantly seeks ways to avoid having to complete them. After dinner, his father asks him to take care of the dishes, as it is his week to do them. Brian says okay but never gets around to them. An hour and a half later, his father comes back and takes all electronics as a result. He removes Brian's tablet, phone, and game system from his room, and as a result, Brian flies into a rage about how those are his own belongings, and they cannot be taken away.

In response, the father with lower EQ skills likely gets just as angry as Brian has. The two of them feed into each other's anger, with it progressing further and further with neither of them being willing to admit fault or blame. Instead, both people refuse to back down, and Brian's father may even resort to doing something he will regret, such as breaking Brian's phone in his rage to prove that he is in charge and can take, or destroy, anything he is paying for. This, of course, only serves to worsen the situation altogether. Brian is far less likely to listen when his own emotions are running high, and if his father cannot control himself, how can Brian really be expected to have the necessary skills to do so?

This entire situation ends with Brian learning that it is acceptable to smash things in his anger, solidifying lower EQ coping mechanisms as acceptable. He never learns how to communicate his own disdain or anger any better, and never learns to be held accountable for his own actions. He sees his father as an adversary rather than a support, and his father has irrevocably damaged his relationship with his son by destroying something belonging to him.

High EQ Father of Teen

Now, imagine Brian's father has a higher EQ. Angry at seeing that his teen has not completed the dishes as expected to, he goes over to his son's room and walks in. Brian is texting someone on his phone instead of getting up. Instead of lashing out angrily, Brian's father calmly tells his son that it is time to do the dishes or there will be consequences. His son seems to shrug it off, not really caring. He once again reiterates the consequences of refusing to do the dishes.

Brian continues to resist doing his chore and instead goes back to his phone. His father nods and walks away to follow through with the consequence. He goes and locks down Wi-Fi and locks Brian's phone on the family plan. Within a minute of his consequence, Brian storms out, yelling about his electronics not working and generally raging.

Brian's father waits for him to finish speaking, and nods, acknowledging that he did disconnect the electronics. He gently reminded his son that nothing in life is free, and if he refuses to go to work, he will not have Wi-Fi or a cell phone to use. His father reiterates that chores must be done, and if Brian refuses to contribute to the household, he will not get the benefits of the household, such as having electronics paid for. He acknowledges how frustrating it is to have to do something that you do not want to do, but enforces the importance of responsibility. He relates to not wanting to go to work to pay for such a high phone bill but doing so out of responsibility and obligation. Adulthood is full of doing things you do not want to do, and it would be best if Brian learned that lesson sooner rather than later.

Brian seems surprised at first but seems to get the idea. He realizes that he has no choice but to contribute and take care of his chores if he wants to continue using his phone. While he may be furious at the results, he sees that there are no other options for him that he wants to go forward with. He begrudgingly does the dishes, learning the lesson of consequences for his actions. He sees that his father did not yell or scream at him, and instead spoke calmly and clearly. He sees the value in properly communicating with his father instead of shouting at him, and learns the valuable lesson of having to do things that you do not want to do, teaching self-management skills. With his high EQ father, he saw emotional intelligence modeled and will be more inclined to follow that example in future conflicts.

19

Assessing the Effectiveness of Your Parenting Style

If you are reading this book, you are probably concerned with your own parenting skills to some degree. You are probably wondering just how effective you are with your parenting, and wondering what you could do to strengthen weaknesses. Luckily for you, this book has your back! This chapter will provide you with a simple questionnaire that you can use to analyze just how effective you are at parenting, as well as providing you with feedback based on how you score and what you can do with that information. The questionnaire is quite short, clocking in at just 50 multiple choice questions, which you will then score after completing them.

What to Expect

This questionnaire is filled with 50 multiple choice questions, each of which is tailored to be easily understood and answered. They will seek to assess just how effective you are at parenting, with a special emphasis on emotion coaching. There will be several questions relating to the five steps of emotion coaching, so you can see which steps you are already skilled at and which you need to work on. If you still feel a little lost about what emotion coaching is and what it entails, do not worry! That is the focus of Part III, which comes right after completing this questionnaire. This assessment is presented first to enable you to comprehend where you stand in terms of effectiveness in the various steps so you can focus on the categories you need the most work on in the next section. Now, whenever you are ready, turn the page to begin the test!

Emotion Coaching Parent Effectiveness Assessment

Welcome to the Emotion Coaching Parent Effectiveness Assessment! This test will analyze and evaluate your effectiveness in regards to the several steps and skills necessary to be an effective emotion coaching parent! Each of these questions will be presented in a multiple-choice format. Be sure to answer each question honestly and carefully to ensure the most accurate results. Remember, this test does not replace the opinion of a licensed professional who understands the ins and outs of your specific situation, and should instead be taken as a general suggestion for how to progress in your journey toward becoming an effective parent as opposed to an expert opinion. Pay special attention to the options of answers, as sometimes, they may change order, or shift from always-never to agree-disagree, or describes me-does not describe me.

When you are ready to begin, make sure you can set aside maybe 15-20 minutes that will be uninterrupted, and bring a piece of paper and a writing utensil, or prepare to record answers on your phone, computer, tablet, or other note-taking apparatus. Focus solely on this assessment without distractions and really consider your answers. Oftentimes, your gut answer will be the most accurate. When writing your answers to your question, record the section, the question number, and the number corresponding to your answer for the easiest grading.

DEVELOPING EMOTIONAL INTELLIGENCE

1. I frequently can tell what my child is thinking or feeling at a glance.

1. Disagree completely	2. Disagree somewhat	3. Neither agree nor disagree	4. Agree somewhat	5. Agree completely

2. My child often gets frustrated with me because I react differently than he or she wants or needs

1. Agree completely	2. Agree somewhat	3. Neither agree nor disagree	4. Disagree somewhat	5. Disagree completely

3. I know what typically triggers my child's negative emotions

1. Disagree completely	2. Disagree somewhat	3. Neither agree nor disagree	4. Agree somewhat	5. Agree completely

4. I can predict when my child is likely to meltdown

1. Never	2. Rarely	3. Sometimes	4. Often	5. Always

5. My child's emotions are difficult for me to understand or recognize. It's like my child is a blank slate and does not emote.

1. Always	2. Often	3. Sometimes	4. Rarely	5. Never

6. I always know exactly what to do to cheer up my child when he or she is feeling sad.

1. Disagree completely	2. Disagree somewhat	3. Neither agree nor disagree	4. Agree somewhat	5. Agree completely

7. My child's emotions seem to catch me by surprise

1. Always	2. Often	3. Sometimes	4. Rarely	5. Never

8. My child trusts that he or she can come to me with anything and know that I will do my best to support him or her.

1. Disagree completely	2. Disagree somewhat	3. Neither agree nor disagree	4. Agree somewhat	5. Agree completely

9. I can name how my child is feeling based on his or her body language.

1. Never	2. Rarely	3. Sometimes	4. Often	5. Always

10. I can often tell there is something wrong with my child, even if he or she says otherwise.

1. Never	2. Rarely	3. Sometimes	4. Often	5. Always

SECTION 1

1. When my child is emotional, I try to walk him or her through what is being felt

| 1. Never | 2. Rarely | 3. Sometimes | 4. Often | 5. Always |

2. When my child does something inappropriate in response to his or her emotions, I:

| 1. Scold him or her for feeling that way. It was unnecessary and unwarranted, and all it did was cause trouble. | 2. Tell him or her to get over it and get his or her act together | 3. Did nothing and allowed my child to feel how he or she wanted | 4. Point out how my child's misbehavior is a problem and tell them not to continue the behaviors. | 5. Point out that it is okay to be upset, but those bad behaviors are unacceptable and offer an alternative behavior. |

3. I encourage my child to consider how his or her behaviors stemming from strong emotions impact other people as well.

| 1. Never | 2. Rarely | 3. Sometimes | 4. Often | 5. Always |

4. I frequently try to vocalize how I am dealing with my own strong emotions when in the presence of my child.

| 1. Disagree completely | 2. Disagree somewhat | 3. Neither agree nor disagree | 4. Agree somewhat | 5. Agree completely |

5. After my child has calmed down, I try to guide him or her through reflecting on the results of strong feelings and the behaviors that came with them to understand the consequences of what happened.

| 1. Never | 2. Rarely | 3. Sometimes | 4. Often | 5. Always |

6. I always encourage my child to reflect upon what happens, good and bad, and identify how things could have been different with different actions.

| 1. Disagree completely | 2. Disagree somewhat | 3. Neither agree nor disagree | 4. Agree somewhat | 5. Agree completely |

7. I want my child to learn from his or her actions and emotions.

| 1. Disagree completely | 2. Disagree somewhat | 3. Neither agree nor disagree | 4. Agree somewhat | 5. Agree completely |

8. My child knows he or she can ask me any questions about feelings and get honest answers from me

| 1. Disagree completely | 2. Disagree somewhat | 3. Neither agree nor disagree | 4. Agree somewhat | 5. Agree completely |

9. Inappropriate behaviors are a natural consequence of negative emotions and should be accepted and allowed as freedom of expression

| 1. Agree completely | 2. Agree somewhat | 3. Neither agree nor disagree | 4. Disagree somewhat | 5. Disagree completely |

10. I make it a personal goal to guide my child through understanding how he or she feels, even if it can be tough at times.

| 1. Disagree completely | 2. Disagree somewhat | 3. Neither agree nor disagree | 4. Agree somewhat | 5. Agree completely |

SECTION 2

DEVELOPING EMOTIONAL INTELLIGENCE

1. I stop what I am doing to hear my child out when he or she comes to me and is visibly upset.

   | 1. Disagree completely | 2. Disagree somewhat | 3. Neither agree nor disagree | 4. Agree somewhat | 5. Agree completely |

2. When my child is crying, I typically acknowledge that and try to relate to a time that I was also upset over something similar.

   | 1. Never | 2. Rarely | 3. Sometimes | 4. Often | 5. Always |

3. My child trusts me enough to come to me in times he or she needs extra emotional support or guidance

   | 1. Disagree completely | 2. Disagree somewhat | 3. Neither agree nor disagree | 4. Agree somewhat | 5. Agree completely |

4. I try to tell my child that getting upset over things is not important and is a waste of time

   | 1. Always | 2. Often | 3. Sometimes | 4. Rarely | 5. Never |

5. When my child is upset or angry, I try to distract them from their emotions.

   | 1. Agree completely | 2. Agree somewhat | 3. Neither agree nor disagree | 4. Disagree somewhat | 5. Disagree completely |

6. I am trying to teach my child to disregard emotions as they are not conducive to rationality.

   | 1. Agree completely | 2. Agree somewhat | 3. Neither agree nor disagree | 4. Disagree somewhat | 5. Disagree completely |

7. I react negatively to my child's emotions.

   | 1. Always | 2. Often | 3. Sometimes | 4. Rarely | 5. Never |

8. My child's emotions are treated as an afterthought, especially if I am busy or if they interfere with what needs to get done.

   | 1. Always | 2. Often | 3. Sometimes | 4. Rarely | 5. Never |

9. I take the time really understand and acknowledge how my child is feeling, no matter how silly it may seem to me

   | 1. Never | 2. Rarely | 3. Sometimes | 4. Often | 5. Always |

10. My child's emotions are always a topic of discussion. I tend to ask how he or she felt about topics that are brought up or about things that happened during the day.

    | 1. Never | 2. Rarely | 3. Sometimes | 4. Often | 5. Always |

SECTION 3

1. I have a wide range of vocabulary to cover various emotions.

   | 1. Disagree completely | 2. Disagree somewhat | 3. Neither agree nor disagree | 4. Agree somewhat | 5. Agree completely |

2. I use a wide range of vocabulary to voice my emotions in ways that other people can understand and try to explain those words to my children.

   | 1. Never | 2. Rarely | 3. Sometimes | 4. Often | 5. Always |

3. Specific words for emotions do not matter, so long as the basic idea is conveyed (e.g., bad or good).

   | 1. Agree completely | 2. Agree somewhat | 3. Neither agree nor disagree | 4. Disagree somewhat | 5. Disagree completely |

4. I seek to voice what my child is feeling in order to instill a better ability to communicate his or her own emotions. For example, if he is crying, I may say he seems so sad or disappointed, depending on the context.

   | 1. Never | 2. Rarely | 3. Sometimes | 4. Often | 5. Always |

5. The more specific the word, the better when it comes to naming emotions

   | 1. Disagree completely | 2. Disagree somewhat | 3. Neither agree nor disagree | 4. Agree somewhat | 5. Agree completely |

6. When someone asks me how I'm feeling, I answer honestly

   | 1. Never | 2. Rarely | 3. Sometimes | 4. Often | 5. Always |

7. I have always struggled to identify and name other people's emotions

   | 1. Agree completely | 2. Agree somewhat | 3. Neither agree nor disagree | 4. Disagree somewhat | 5. Disagree completely |

8. I can clearly identify and differentiate between similar emotions, and am teaching my child to do so as well (e.g., guilt vs. shame or pride vs. happiness)

   | 1. Disagree completely | 2. Disagree somewhat | 3. Neither agree nor disagree | 4. Agree somewhat | 5. Agree completely |

9. I understand what people mean when they list specific emotions (e.g., feeling ecstatic or despair).

   | 1. Never | 2. Rarely | 3. Sometimes | 4. Often | 5. Always |

10. I struggle to communicate my emotions verbally.

    | 1. Agree completely | 2. Agree somewhat | 3. Neither agree nor disagree | 4. Disagree somewhat | 5. Disagree completely |

SECTION 4

DEVELOPING EMOTIONAL INTELLIGENCE

1. I let my child flounder and fail when confronted with adversity, and do not intervene, no matter how bad the situation may get.

1. Agree completely	2. Agree somewhat	3. Neither agree nor disagree	4. Disagree somewhat	5. Disagree completely

2. When my child is facing a problem, I ask guiding questions to help lead him or her to potential solutions.

1. Never	2. Rarely	3. Sometimes	4. Often	5. Always

3. If my child is struggling, I will take over completely to ensure he or she does not fail.

1. Always	2. Often	3. Sometimes	4. Rarely	5. Never

4. My child should never experience failure. Failure is a sign of weakness and incompetence and should be looked down upon.

1. Agree completely	2. Agree somewhat	3. Neither agree nor disagree	4. Disagree somewhat	5. Disagree completely

5. Adversity and problem-solving build character, even if failure happens, and I encourage and welcome that for my child.

1. Disagree completely	2. Disagree somewhat	3. Neither agree nor disagree	4. Agree somewhat	5. Agree completely

6. I will tell my child exactly what to do to fix a problem without making him or her come up with the answer.

1. Agree completely	2. Agree somewhat	3. Neither agree nor disagree	4. Disagree somewhat	5. Disagree completely

7. My child is learning the value in failing in controlled environments where I can intervene if necessary.

1. Disagree completely	2. Disagree somewhat	3. Neither agree nor disagree	4. Agree somewhat	5. Agree completely

8. My child is encouraged to think of solutions to problems underneath my supervision and is welcome to ask for help if necessary.

1. Disagree completely	2. Disagree somewhat	3. Neither agree nor disagree	4. Agree somewhat	5. Agree completely

9. When I am faced with my own conflict around my child, I make it a point to talk out how I am solving it so my children can see what good problem-solving skills look like.

1. Never	2. Rarely	3. Sometimes	4. Often	5. Always

10. My child is encouraged to see failure as a learning experience and not something to be embarrassed or self-conscious about.

1. Disagree completely	2. Disagree somewhat	3. Neither agree nor disagree	4. Agree somewhat	5. Agree completely

SECTION 5

Calculating Your Scores

Congratulations! You have finished the questionnaire! Now for the fun part—calculating your score. Luckily for you, this questionnaire had ease of scoring in mind. Each answer should be scored as the number of the answer subtracting 1. So if you chose answer 4, you would award 3 points for that question in that section.

Answer 1	0 points
Answer 2	1 point
Answer 3	2 points
Answer 4	3 points
Answer 5	4 points

For further ease, you could add up the sum of all answers within your section and subtract 10 (1 point per question) from the final result to get your score per section. When you have your category scores, you can begin to identify what your scores mean for you. Each section of the assessment related to a different emotion coaching skill.

Section 1	Awareness of Child's Feelings
Section 2	Seeing Emotions as Teaching Experiences
Section 3	Listening and Validating Child's Emotions
Section 4	Labeling Emotions
Section 5	Encouraging Problem-Solving

Your results

This table shows how you should expect your results to be calculated. You can look at this table at a glance to see which category each of your skill levels fell into, as well as seeing how your general effectiveness holds up.

Result	Individual Emotion Coaching Skill Effectiveness	Total Emotion Coaching Effectiveness
Area for Enrichment: Needs work	0-24	0-120
Effective Functioning: Proficient, but could be strengthened	25-34	121-170
Enhanced: Highly effective	35-40	171-200

Area for Enrichment (0-24 individual skill effectiveness, or 0-120 general effectiveness)

In this category, you show that you are struggling to parent in a way that is reminiscent of emotion coaching. You likely are not very in control of the situation when one arises, and you may struggle to help your child process emotions healthily. You, yourself, likely have some sort of impaired level of emotional intelligence, and likely find yourself losing your temper frequently when interacting with emotionally volatile children.

This can lead to a lot of tension with your child, as your child never gets the support needed to develop healthily. You struggle to emulate skills your child would learn through watching you, never giving your children the foundation that would make functioning throughout adulthood far easier. Your child is likely to pick up negative coping mechanisms or attitudes surrounding emotions, especially for negative emotions, and this can lead to many issues overall. Your child may struggle to

If you score in this category for either individual skills or as a whole, you need to work on your emotion coaching to become more effective. The most effective way to go about this would be seeking out books about strengthening your own emotional intelligence. There are two other books in this series: *Emotional Intelligence 2.0* and *Emotional Intelligence Practical Guide* that could work help you with that process. By raising your own emotional intelligence, you will find that the skills involved in emotion coaching come easier.

If you struggle with only one or two skills in emotion coaching, then you should seek to bolster it with your other skills. For example, if you are great at seeing emotions as learning experiences, but you struggle with encouraging problem-solving, you can work to use your skills at making things learning experiences to start looking at problems as more learning experiences. By shifting your expectation and mindset, you may be better able to encourage problem-solving, as problem-solving itself becomes a learning experience in your mind. Instead of seeing it as your child failing, you would see your child learning. Come up with ways that your stronger skills can strengthen and support your weaknesses, and you may find yourself performing better with emotion coaching.

Effective Functioning (25-34 individual skill effectiveness, or 121-170 general effectiveness)

If you fall into this category, your skills are at the very least functional. You can emotion-coach well enough, but you likely still struggle sometimes, especially with some of your weaker skills. There is always room for improvement, and you should consider any skills that fall within this category as worthy of revisiting and attempting to better, but they will do in a pinch.

If you are effective at emotion coaching, you are likely pretty average in terms of your own EQ as well. You are content in your life, though you may run into roadblocks that you struggle to overcome sometimes. You may run into bumps, especially with your children, as you try to guide them through the messiness that is their emotional state. Because you, yourself, do not have a mastery over your own emotional control, you may make mistakes frequently, though you likely admit to them and apologize to your child for them as well.

As a parent, you can probably navigate through day-to-day emotions just fine with your children, and you find coaching them during mild anger, sadness, or fear easy enough, you likely struggle as soon as emotions are heightened, as they often are with children. You may fail to communicate effectively enough to really prevent most arguments or backlash, and you likely also may fail at really defusing the tensest emotional situations effectively.

If you have scored within this range, your skills will suffice, but you should seek to strengthen them over time. Keep practicing those skills until you become more effective! Likewise, look into strengthening your EQ! You always have room to improve!

Enhanced Skill (35-40 individual skill effectiveness, or 171-200 general effectiveness)

Congratulations! This is the best score category you could have achieved! If your scores have fallen within this range, you have a near-mastery of the skill you tested. You are effective and efficient in the skills that scored at this level, and you are likely extremely efficient at emotion coaching in general.

This has great connotations for your children—they are likely getting the best upbringing they could from you. You are preparing them for the real world and creating a foundation of emotional intelligence. You are giving them the skills that they will need to set themselves up for success in the future.

If you scored within this range for emotion coaching in general, you are likely within a high range for your own emotional intelligence. You probably manage to guide your children through difficult situations with relative ease, and frequently are able to settle conflicts quickly and maturely, something your child appreciates. You are likely quite empathetic with your children, and always consider their own emotions when approaching or parenting them. If you have scored within this range, keep up the good work and make sure you continue to practice such good emotion coaching skills!

20

Emotion Coaching Elements

There are several various elements to emotion coaching that arise as recurring themes to the skill. Within the five steps, these elements should be present. These elements help keep both yourself and your child in line, as well as set the stage for the steps of emotion coaching to run its course in the most effective manner. The four most important elements underlying emotion coaching are:

1. Unconditional Love
2. Providing Ample Space
3. Mentoring relationships
4. Healthy Boundaries

Unconditional Love

Every child needs love to grow and develop. It is so inherently important that many of the interactions with young children and their parents are designed to biologically create a deep bond between the two. It has literally been ingrained in our instincts to fiercely love and protect our children from anything that may threaten their survival or success. Unconditional love is love that will be there no matter what. It is the idea that nothing your child could do would ever diminish or mar the love you feel toward him or her.

This is an incredibly important foundation in emotion coaching; by providing your child with unconditional love, he or she learns that any communication and any expression of emotion is acceptable to you, so long as it is verbal. Your child knows that, even when acting out, or making mistakes, you will not love your child any less. This is an important foundation of trust.

Through trusting you, your child will be more willing to heed advice, and more inclined to go to you when she needs help, even if it is her own fault that she is in the mess she has gotten herself into, such as she decided to drink at a party and now is afraid to drive home. A teen with trust in her parents' unconditional love is likely to call and ask for a ride home, knowing just how dangerous driving home after drinking could be. This is a good thing—it means your child has developed coping skills and knows she can communicate with you.

Providing Ample Space

Teaching your child how to manage problems is important. For this reason, you must give your child the space necessary to make mistakes in order to teach him how to solve them. If your child never makes mistakes, he is never in a position where he has to fix things, meaning he never develops crucial skills that he will need in adulthood. If you solve every problem for your child as they come up, all your child learns is that you will always be there to bail him out—but what happens when you are no longer there? Every person dies at some point, and if you were to have an untimely death late in your child's teen years or early into adulthood, he would not have the skills he would need to survive socially.

No parent enjoys seeing their child suffer; however, it is an important part of growing up. Instead of being afraid of your child failing, you should be recognizing that failing is a necessary step toward succeeding. There are plenty of things that are failed dozens of times, or even hundreds, or thousands, or countless times before someone succeeds. Think of landing on the moon; that was once an impossibility, but now it is commonly accepted as doable. You must be able to provide your child with the space necessary to explore and develop important skills.

By having the space necessary to develop individually, your child is working on foundations for problem-solving and communicating effectively with peers. These skills are invaluable and absolutely necessary to be a successful adult.

Mentoring Relationships

Rather than seeing the parent-child relationship as the parent being in a position of power or authority over the child, or seeing the parent-child relationship as a friendship, you should aim to create a mentoring relationship between the two of you. Within a mentoring relationship, you acknowledge that you are teaching and guiding your child rather than controlling and asserting authority over her. She needs to be treated as her own individual rather than controlled. She is her own person and will have her own likes, dislikes, emotions, and preferences. Your job is to ensure she has the social skills and emotional intelligence to cope with whatever life throws at her while allowing her to flourish into whoever she was destined to be.

By keeping your relationship in terms of a mentorship rather than one built on the authority vested in you simply because you are the parent, you will be in a better mindset. Your job is to teach, not command.

You will keep your interactions with your child tailored to inform how best to act rather than requiring it. Just as you can lead a horse to water, but can never force it to drink, you cannot force your child to follow through with what you have suggested. The best you can do is hope that your modeling and teaching have paid off and your child has heeded your suggestion.

Healthy Boundaries

Every relationship requires healthy boundaries, and the parent-child relationship is no exception. While your child should feel comfortable coming to talk to you in confidence about anything, that should not be reciprocal. You should not be burdening your child with your own heavy thoughts or feelings, especially if those things are relevant to your child's other parent. You should not try to make your child your own confidante. While it is true that you should be open and honest, you should stick to facts rather than giving the child details that he has no business knowing.

Likewise, there should be boundaries the other way as well. Your child needs to develop independence somewhere, and you need to make sure that you give your child all the privacy he or she requests, so long as it is safe to do so. Most teens will be fine with that sort of privacy, barring any other physical or mental health issues, and you need to give that to them. As your child will hopefully eventually enter the world on his or her own, you need to respect desires for boundaries or privacy, as well, which further gives your child the chance to begin mastering managing emotions and solving problems, two of the important parts of emotional intelligence. Children who are given the reins while still being guided by you are far more likely to be successful than children who are constantly directed, or children who do not receive any real guidance at all. Toeing that fine line between following, crossing, and not coming close enough to the boundary is difficult, but is worthwhile when it comes to your child's emotional intelligence.

Common Emotion Coaching Mistakes

Within emotion coaching, several mistakes can happen pretty frequently. It should come as no surprise—emotion coaching is just as much of a series of skills as emotional intelligence is, and it requires practice to get right. No parent is magically fantastic at emotion coaching, and no parent ever gets it perfectly from the get-go without ever making mistakes at some point. Perfection and humans do not go hand in hand, and you should not feel bad about making any of these mistakes. Instead, just as you teach your children, look at your mistakes as learning opportunities and aim to avoid making them in the future as well. With practice and perseverance, you will get it.

1. Overly-permissive

If one of the important elements of emotion coaching is providing space for the child to develop and grow on his or her own, it should come as no surprise that people often overcorrect and grant their children too much freedom. Oftentimes, this can be done with good intentions, but they do say that the road to hell is paved with them. No matter how well-meaning you may have been, your child needs guidance somewhere. Yes, your child should be allowed to make mistakes and flounder now and again, but you do not leave your child to flounder alone. You need to be there to catch your child before he is seriously hurt. You are still there to guide your child, even if you are not micro-managing. Think of this as supervising your young child at the playground—you are there if your child needs you, but not constantly trying to tell him how to play or what to do or say. You would not allow your young child to try to climb on the outside of the slide that is 15 feet tall and would likely intervene if you saw your child trying to. You should take that same sort of stance with your child in other aspects of life as well, allowing him to experiment and explore, but drawing a line where lines must be drawn for safety's sake.

If you know that your child is engaging in unsafe sex, for example, you should not allow that to continue. While you cannot necessarily police a teen's sex life, nor can you control your teen at all hours of every day, you can step in, have the safe sex talk, and offer to take the teen to get birth control and provide condoms. This is not overly controlling—this is teaching your child life-long lessons and ensuring that she does not do something that could have permanent repercussions for her, such as having a child as a teen or catching an STI. Teaching your child about safe sexual practices, consent, and birth control is well within the normal realm for parenting responsibilities, and not having those conversations would border on neglectful.

2. Solving the problem for the child

Remember how not helping the child at all was a problem and lead to the child struggling to solve problems at all? Well, doing all of the work is another common overcorrection. People may feel as though they are too permissive and overcorrect by not allowing the child any opportunities to attempt solving the problem at all. Parents may insert themselves where they are unwanted or unwarranted, rather than allowing their children room to grow. These children grow to be overly dependent on their parents and generally incapable of managing life on their own.

Frequently, their peers look down upon them due to their stunted nature, and no one wants to befriend the person with the emotional maturity of someone several years younger than them. Especially once your child goes off to college, if that is something he chooses to do, he is going to struggle greatly if you have spent his entire life working things out for him. He needs to have the chance to grow on his own without parental involvement since it is really only the first 20% or so of a person's life that they require such intensive involvement from another person. Especially as your teen gets through the middle-late teen years, he needs to experience the consequences of failure. If he needs his gym shorts clean for the next day but left them in the washer overnight, do not move them for him; let him suffer the consequences when he wakes up and finds them sopping wet and smelling like mildew the next morning. He needs to learn to rely on himself to prepare for the real world. Likewise, if he chooses not to write a paper, do not provide him with an out, an excused absence, or even help him write it. Let him suffer the repercussions, even if it leaves a mark on his grades or he winds up unable to play in his basketball game due to academic problems.

3. Unhealthy or nonexistent boundaries

Boundaries are important. That has been established already. However, those boundaries have to be healthy. Unhealthy boundaries, such as boundaries that are far too strict, or nonexistent boundaries, can actually prove to be emotionally harmful rather than beneficial. It can be difficult to mind the balance between them, and far too often, parents stray too far from that find line and into the territory of unhealthy boundaries.

When dealing with unhealthy boundaries, the parent may put far too much emphasis on the child listening to conversations that are inappropriate, such as about the parent's relationships, or other unreasonable topics of conversation. This can lead to a child feeling as though she must be the emotional support for her parent rather than the other way around. This is unhealthy and robs the child of innocence, forcing her to grow up far too early. If a child frequently listens to her mother complain about her father or other relationships, the mother is putting the child in a role where she feels obligated to emotionally support and care for her mother, even though that is none of her concern and likely inappropriate. This child learns to push away her own emotions in favor of other people's and never really learns self-regulation skills.

On the other hand, children whose parents have boundaries that are far too strict, such as a parent who does not wish to hear any emotional discussion, grow up feeling undervalued. A parent who puts up boundaries that are too strict leaves a child feeling as though they are missing parts of those close bonds typically developed with parents. Instead, the child feels the need to seek that bond out elsewhere, and may even engage in riskier behaviors seeking out the relationship that should have been developed with the parents. This child may seek out romantic relationships, even if they are unhealthy, just to feel close to someone if that role is not being fulfilled by parents. This can also lead to early exposure to all sorts of topics and things that children or teens have no business experimenting with. Likewise, this child is not likely to learn the skills necessary to self-regulate or to interact appropriately with other people. Because the child's parent instead prefers to keep the relationship within strict terms and may never allow the child to experiment beyond what the parent dictates, the child never learns how to interact with others or communicate when he may feel like needs are not being met.

4. Too strict

Sometimes, parents try to parent but only manage to be too strict instead. Rather than creating a safe, controlled environment for their children to learn, they instead crackdown so there is never anything to learn. Their children may never be allowed to play with certain crowds due to misperceptions, or may not get the chance to go to sleepovers or parties due to their parents thinking they are inappropriate. They may be denied the ability to date during the teen years when children are learning all about their preferences and how to be in romantic relationships while still having the guidance of parents.

These children miss out on many aspects of social development that are crucial to learning all aspects of emotional intelligence. When they finally are old enough to break free into the real world, they are often severely emotionally stunted, and may even overcorrect, experimenting with everything they were denied in childhood. They likely lack control over themselves as being in control was never an option. Since their parents dictated everything, they never learned to make proper decisions or face the consequences of poor decisions as children when the long-term effects are typically minimal compared to having them happen in adulthood. Consider a teen who gets into a fight and impulsively punches someone—that will go on his record, and he may get in some trouble, but he is a minor and the criminal records of minors are typically considered confidential. However, if that same teen punches someone at age 19 shortly after moving out, that is considered a crime committed in adulthood and becomes public record, marring his background check for the next several years. By being too strict, you do your child a disservice. Your child needs to learn how to self-regulate and control himself while risks are still low. As a child and a teen, those risks are at the lowest they will ever be.

21

Emotion Coaching Strategies

Emotion coaching is an integral part of raising emotionally intelligent children. It is the middle step between coaching elements and emotional intelligence.

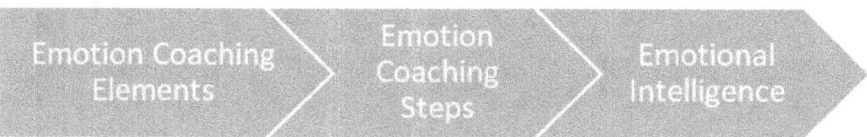

Without emotion coaching, children do not receive the best foundations for building high EQs. While growing up in homes without emotion, coaching does not necessarily doom a child to failure as an adult; it certainly does not do the child any favors. He can grow to be quite emotionally intelligent despite his upbringing, but his upbringing is not what caused it unless he chose to be the exact opposite of what he was exposed to throughout life.

What is Emotion Coaching?

Simply put, emotion coaching is a type of communication strategy. It is meant to support children and teens while they develop their own emotional intelligence and learn how to manage their own relationships. This parenting strategy teaches children to understand their own emotions, as well as how to manage them and cope in productive ways. Five steps come together to create effective, successful emotion coaching. These are:

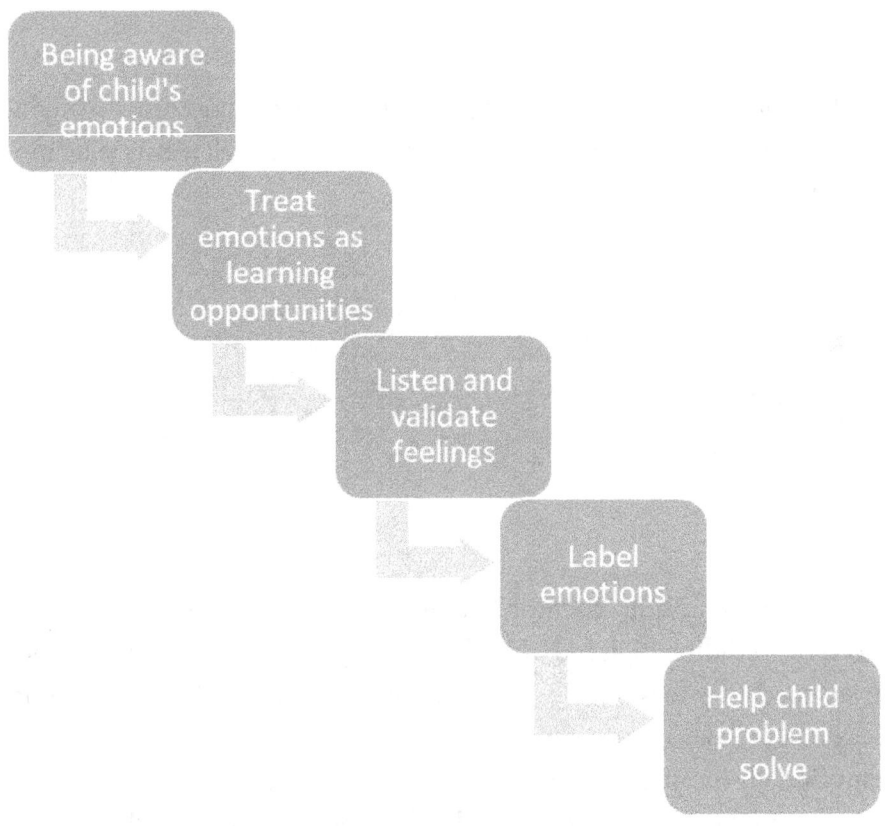

When all five steps come together, skillfully, a parenting style with an emphasis on empathy and developing higher levels of emotional intelligence is born. It is a very intensive parenting style and requires higher levels of patience and time, but that effort is well worth it when your

DEVELOPING EMOTIONAL INTELLIGENCE

child becomes more prepared for the adversities that will be faced in the future, as well as when you notice your own relationship with the child improving.

Step 1: Be Aware of Your Child's Emotions (and Your Own!)

Emotional intelligence is, as implied, all about emotions. Of course, the foundation is having a general knowledge of emotions. Just as the foundation to emotional intelligence is self-awareness, you must be aware of your child's emotions to be able to effectively emotion coach. An effective emotion coach must be a master at their own self-regulation. Pay attention to your own emotions first, no matter what they are, and understand them. Likewise, you should pay attention to your child's emotions, as well. Pay special attention to how your child expresses himself in various contexts with different emotions. You need to learn your child's emotional expressions if you hope to coach him. Watch for body language and facial expressions that can be helpful in the future to help you understand how your child is feeling at a glance. This will be crucial when you attempt to emotion coach.

If you are struggling with identifying your own emotions, it would be prudent to first work on strengthening your own self-awareness before proceeding. Remember, emotion coaching requires plenty of emotional intelligence from the parent's part to succeed; if you are struggling to identify your own feelings and emotional tells on the regular, you will struggle to accurately read your child's as well.

To see how this step might play out, consider this example: If you see your child in a tough situation, you may notice how his brow furrows in frustration, paired with a small scowl while his whole body tenses up as he stares intently at whatever happens to be frustrating him. You may notice how you can see the frustration in his eyes, and then you see him stomp his feet and clench his fists as he tries to figure out what to do to solve his frustration. His voice may be sharper when he talks, or he may whine and say he is stuck and needs help. The longer you focus on your child's body language, you may begin to identify smaller cues to their emotional state, such as the way he may bite his lip when scared or how one eyebrow may be quirked slightly when puzzled. Watch for patterns until you understand the ins and outs of your child's body language.

With a teen, this may be a bit more difficult. Teens are prone to sulking around by their nature and may even focus on hiding their emotions and coming across as cool and collected at all times. Even with teens, you may be able to notice emotional tells. Maybe her voice quivers slightly when she is upset, or she tends to play with her hair when nervous. Even teens who try their best likely have some emotional tells that you will be able to identify if you focus long enough on trying to discover them.

Step 2: See Emotions as Teaching and Learning Opportunities

Remember how with emotional intelligence, learning opportunities come from failure? Well, they also come from emotions in general! Especially when emotions and tensions run high, you might make mistakes. It takes a lot of self-management to be able to regulate your own reactions, especially if the emotions being felt are negative.

You likely will struggle with this step if you struggle with self-management for yourself. You need to be able to control your own emotions and reactions if you hope to be able to recommend ways to manage your child's, especially if your child's emotions are directed your way. It is easy to feel frustrated if your child is screaming, "I hate you!" over and over again in his anger about you refusing to allow him to eat dessert before dinner, after all.

Once again, within this step, you want to pay close attention to how your child is feeling. When emotions start running high, this is your cue to start a learning moment. You can identify your child's feeling to him, putting a word to those strong feelings that your child may not fully understand, depending on the age. You can provide your child with ways to cope with his strong emotions as well, guiding him through the steps one by one.

For example, if your six-year-old son is crying inconsolably because he dropped his Lego masterpiece that he spent all afternoon building and broke it, you have the perfect opportunity to guide your child through that disappointment and dismay. You should approach your child and get on your child's level. Put a hand on his shoulder and tell him that he looks very frustrated and sad right now, and ask if he wants a hug. Respect whatever his answer is to that question, and follow up with something along the lines of, "Are you frustrated?" Wait for him to answer. "Do you know what I do when I'm upset like you are? I like to take a deep breath, hold it in, count to five, and then breathe out as hard as I can. Would you like to try to do that too?" Gently urge your child to go along with your method. If he is reluctant, do not push, but stay there with your child and try offering another method to calm down. "What if you stomp three times? Would you feel better then?" If your child refuses to try, there is not much you can do other than be there for him. While you should not punish your child, suggesting that your child takes a private moment to compose himself is acceptable if what he wants to do is cry it out. The goal here is to guide your child to cope with emotions before he escalates from being upset into misbehaving or acting out. Crying on its own is not a form of acting out, and you should never tell your child not to cry or not to be a crybaby. If your child starts to calm down, you can ask him to talk about what happened and why he feels the way he does in order to encourage him to speak about his emotions.

With a teen, this step is often a bit more difficult. Teens are far more standoffish than children most of the time and maybe far more reluctant to speak about emotions with parents. Nevertheless, you should still seek to encourage it. If your teen comes home, seeming a little more reserved and brooding than usual, you can ask him what happened. Be prepared for the answer to be that nothing happened and everything is fine, and remember not to pry, no matter how much you may want to.

Gently remind your teen that you are there if he wants to talk and move on. If his emotions begin to impact other people, such as snapping at people at the dinner table, gently call your child to the task and remind him that snapping is not acceptable, but that he is welcome to talk to you about whatever is bothering him. If he firmly refuses to speak to you, you can also encourage emotional expression through journaling or encouraging him to talk to friends, or even offering a therapist if you notice that his emotions are getting out of hand.

Step 3: Listen and Validate Your Child's Feelings

Step 3 requires you to use two skills to better help your child: both empathy and listening skills. It takes a lot of effort to really listen and comprehend what someone else is saying, and that skill is something that many people have to go out of their way to strengthen. If listening skills are something you struggle with, work on those while also attempting this step. That is a skill that will serve you well, and will also benefit your child as well.

In order to validate your child's feelings, you must make it a point to take what she says seriously. Do not dismiss or criticize her emotions, as that only serves to make her feel invalidated, and misses the entire point of this step. Emotions, no matter what they are, are valid if they are being felt. There are no right or wrong ways to feel in certain situations, and you need to respect and remember that. If your child approaches you with specific feelings, you should always acknowledge and accept it. Further, you should make it a point to show your child that you are listening and even try to paraphrase what she says to you to ensure that you understand. By repeating back what she has said to you, you give her the opportunity to correct any misunderstandings.

Consider your 5-year-old daughter coming up to you and saying, "I'm really disappointed you didn't take me to the part today like we always do on Mondays." She might look up at you and pout. Your gut reaction may be to react defensively. Yes, you may typically take her to the park Monday evenings, but that particular day, you had had a late meeting at work, and then traffic had been horrendous on the way home, and you may have been an hour and a half late, eating into the time you would usually use for the park. Instead, you should seek to understand what your child is saying. Tell her that you understand and that you are also disappointed that you could not go to the park today, and ask if the two of you can go tomorrow instead.

Maybe your teenager comes up to you and says he is annoyed that you keep making him do chores and that he has to turn in his electronics by 10pm on school nights. He may try to make the argument that his friend has no curfew or chores, so he should not be required to do those things because it is not fair. He vents these frustrations to you and then asks you to eliminate the requirements.

This is a tricky situation, as disagreeing with him may come across as invalidating his emotions. This situation requires tact and skillful communication. You can respond saying that you were also frustrated by having to do chores as a child. Remind him that you are not his friend's parent and that your house rules stand, no matter how frustrating they may be for him. Acknowledge his feelings as valid and that he is more than welcome to feel that way, but those feelings do not obligate you to change your rules, no matter how unfair he may feel it is. Remind him that when he is an adult and in his own home, he is more than welcome to set his own rules, but for now, he has to live with yours.

Step 4: Label Emotions

Step 4 returns back to the basics: self-awareness. Thus far, you have noticed your child's emotions, made it a point to acknowledge your child's feelings, and listened to what your child has had to say about his or her feelings without invalidating them, and now it is time to aid your child in identifying how she may feel. With this step, you should seek to name your child's emotions, identifying the emotions you can see present, and encouraging your child to use emotional vocabulary.

Putting a name to the feeling makes it less overwhelming and less intimidating. It allows your child to know exactly what she is dealing with. Much how knowing exactly what to expect is less frustrating or upsetting than being blindsided, your child being able to name exactly what she is feeling will take away some of the lack of control she may be feeling.

This step should also be followed for yourself: Name your emotions to your child as you feel them to set the example and help your child understand that emotions are normal and acceptable, while also helping your child develop a good vocabulary for the emotions she is likely to encounter.

Consider your four-year-old child throwing a tantrum over having gotten the wrong color plate. Perhaps he had asked for the pink one, but you did not hear him and gave the pink plate to his younger brother instead. This has set your four-year-old off, and he is crying about the color while insisting his brother gives him the plate, even though the two plates have entirely different food, with his brother's missing the foods that tend to upset his stomach that your four-year-old loves to eat.

Get down to his level and say, "I can see that you are very frustrated at the moment, aren't you?" He will probably nod his head angrily in response. "I'm sorry that I didn't hear you ask for pink—how about you take the pink plate for dinner? But for now, your brother is eating his food, and you can't take his plate away. I'm sorry you are so upset and frustrated, but frustration is not a good reason to make your brother stop eating. That would make him sad and frustrated, too." He may or may not agree to wait until dinner for the pink plate, but no matter the result, you have encouraged him to think about the word frustrated.

With a teen, things will probably be a bit more nuanced. If your teen comes to you and is acting out, snapping at everyone, you may ask why he is so irritated in the hopes of finding out what his problem is. He may shrug you off and not give you an answer, but at the very least, you have put a name to his feeling, or at least, what you are assuming is his feeling. You are far more likely to get results with internalizing good usage of emotional terms by dictating your own feelings: "I feel really frustrated when you snap at everyone like that. Can we use kinder words and tones instead?"

Step 5: Encourage Problem Solving

This step is all about fixing problems before they get out of hand. You should correct your children's misbehaviors while making sure that you are emphasizing that the behavior is the problem, not the emotion. You can do this by explaining why the behavior is wrong. Emphasize that emotions should be expressed, but through words, not through acting out. This is a good time to start offering solutions for how to fix the problem as well. Keep in mind that it takes time to teach children to think critically about problems and begin identifying solutions, but it is a skill that is crucial to learn. It may be easier to tell your kid how to fix things, but that will not serve her as well in the long run. Instead, encouraging her to explore solutions with your supervision is a much better option. Further, when teaching your child to problem solve, make it a point to praise your child whenever she does something well or solves a problem on her own, so she knows she is on the right track.

Assume that your 6-year-old daughter is upset because her younger brother accidentally knocked over the big block castle she has been building. You hear her scream, "No!" and hear the sound of blocks flying, and your younger child comes running away, crying and clutching his head. Your daughter threw a block at him because he knocked down her castle.

In this situation, you should go to your child and identify that it is okay to be frustrated and angry, but throwing blocks is not safe and not acceptable under any circumstances. Point out how throwing the block hurt her brother and made him cry, and ask her if she knows what she should do next. At this point, she may apologize and say she can build it again, or she may dig in her heels and refuse to make any changes to her behavior. If she does not want to change her behavior, you could try sending her to time out until she is ready to behave, as children who are not ready to be nice do not need to be spending time with others.

Imagine that your teen has come home, upset about having failed a test. You know that the night prior to the test, he had spent the day playing video games, and then spent the night sleeping. He hadn't even attempted to study at all, and you know it. Upset, he tells you that he's so stupid and that he's never going to be able to go to the college he really wants to attend.

You ask him what happened with the test, and he says he does not know. You ask if he studied and see him look away sheepishly. You ask again, and he answers honestly; he did not think he needed to study because he had felt confident about the material. Then, you can ask him what he could do next time to make sure he has the appropriate amount of time to study, and you see the realization click. He seems to have gotten the idea.

22

Emotion Coaching as Your Child Grows

10 Tips for Being Aware of Your Child or Teen's Emotions

1. Take a few moments every time you interact with your child to really study their expressions and put them in context with what is happening at that moment. Does she cross her arms when she is annoyed? Does he scrunch up his face when he smiles when he's ecstatic? Learn the subtle difference between both positive and negative emotions.
2. Notice how your child holds his or her body in a wide range of situations and seek to find patterns in posture based on emotions. Does he stand up straight and tall when proud or happy? Does she seem to try to shrink back when sad or frightened? Does he seem combatant when angry?
3. Listen to your child's voice and search for undertones that will let you cue into your child's emotional state. Does her voice waver when she is sad? Is there a squeal in her words when he is thrilled to be somewhere or doing something? Can you hear the uncertainty in his words when he doesn't know what to do next?
4. Look for little quirks or habits your child has when feeling certain ways, such as biting nails when nervous or twirling hair when restless. These can tell you far more than words, especially if your child happens to have a few telltale quirks, such as shifting feet

back and forth or being unable to sit still when caught being dishonest.

5. Take the time to study your child's face when he or she is sleeping to get a clear idea of what the child's relaxed face looks like. Especially if your child has not slept with you for a while, it may look different than you remember! Take the few moments to really study that sleeping face and see how his features soften compared to what you are used to seeing during the day.

6. Learn to speak your teen's body language: Try to catch onto slightly different postures or expressions your teen may have that will help you cue into their emotional state. Teens are typically much more reserved with their emotions, so learning subtleties in your teen's body language is likely one of your best bets to understand how he is feeling.

7. Pay attention to whatever your teen is emphasizing at that moment. Some teens will journal or write obsessively during tough times, while others may play different types of video games depending on mood. Sometimes, they will play the music that closely relates to how they are feeling as well. Pay attention to how your teen is spending his time when at home.

8. No matter how tempting it may be, DO NOT try to take your teen's diary or journal, or otherwise invade your teen's privacy unless you have a good reason to do so. Yes, you would be able to learn what is happening and where your teen stands emotionally, but that is a significant betrayal of trust and will do far more damage than good.

9. Try to identify the undertones when your teen does open up with you. Listen to the language that is being used—is it self-deprecating, or is it playful and confident? Is it inherently angry or more positive and optimistic? You can learn a lot about people by hearing the undertones behind the words, or paying attention to the context.

10. Watch how your teen interacts with peers (from afar, of course!). If your friend invites friends over, try to stay out of the way while paying attention to how she seems to interact with her friends. Are they happily chatting away, giggling, and enjoying each other's company? Do they seem upset or depressed? Do you see anything that is inherently worrying when she hangs out with her friends? This may be the most honest picture of your child's emotional states you will get, as she is bound to be more expressive with her friends than with her family at this stage.

10 Tips for Approaching Your Child or Teen's Emotions as Learning Opportunities

1. When something goes wrong when your child is trying to do something, ask her how she feels about that, and encourage him to be as expressive or descriptive as possible. You may need to add guiding questions in here, such as asking if angry is all she feels, or if there is more than one emotion bothering her at that moment. You want her to be as honest as possible with you, and you want her to practice using as many descriptive words as she can to foster communication skills.
2. Ask your child to think about how he could turn that negative event into something positive and productive instead. If his drawing does not quite look like a dragon, maybe he could turn it into something else and create a story about it instead of focusing on failing at attaining perfection. This reminds your child that imperfection can still be great or inspiring and that there is always light to find in a situation, even if it did not turn out the way your child may have expected. This also teaches your child to be flexible.
3. Make a cake with your child. Hype it up as being the most delicious cake and make it a point to let your child help you decorate. When you give her the first slice, ask her to smash the cake with a spatula. When she does, ask her to take a bite of it, and then ask if it is still good, even though it was no longer exactly what she expected.
4. When watching a movie with your child, ask him to identify the feelings of other characters. Ask why they feel that way. Encourage your child to be as descriptive as he can be with the emotions in order to foster a wider emotional vocabulary. Encourage him to try this at key emotional points in the movie with a wide range of characters. Not only does this get him thinking about

emotions, but it also encourages him to exercise his brain through analysis and comprehension.
5. Ask your child to imagine how she would feel if she were in another character's shoes when watching a TV show. This encourages her to think empathetically, imagining whether she would react similarly, or try an entirely different approach. Ask her to explain her reasoning as she does this as clearly as she can manage.
6. Encourage your teen to consider how his emotionally fueled actions impacted a friend or family member. You want him to identify how his own actions can impact many people around him as well, even if he did not intend to do so.
7. The next time you are upset at your teen, turn it into an empathy exercise. Ask her to identify your feelings, and to do her best to explain why you feel that way. Turn this into a discussion with you telling her how you actually feel and the reason behind it if your teen's guess was wrong.
8. Attempt to identify people's thoughts, feelings, and emotions at a glance to pass the time while driving or traveling with your teen. He has to look at someone, say how he is feeling, and offer up a reason for it, either humorous, or serious, and you have to decide whether it is realistic, and vice versa.
9. The next time your teen has a large outburst, encourage her to reflect upon it, judgment-free after tensions have fallen. Explain that you are happy to listen, so long as your teen is mindful of her emotions and is not lashing out or hurting other people.
10. The next time you and your teen witness an altercation or argument, ask your teen what he would do to avoid being in a situation like that. He does not necessarily have to answer out loud, but you want him to start thinking about tough emotional issues.

10 Tips for Listening to and Validating Your Child or Teen's Emotions

1. Always make eye contact and put down distractions when your child or teen approaches you. Make it a point to give your child or teen your undivided attention. This teaches your child good listening skills while also proving that you care enough to put away any of the distractions and spend some good one-on-one time with your child. Your child deserves your full attention when she comes to you to talk about emotions, even if it may be at an inconvenient time.
2. Always paraphrase your teen or child's words back to him to ensure you heard him correctly. It can be difficult to fully understand what a child or teen is saying, especially if he is still young and struggles to fully articulate himself. If you did not understand your child correctly, he has the opportunity to correct you before the conversation progresses any further. If you have understood correctly, you proved to your child that you are actively listening.
3. When your child or teen approaches you to speak, make sure that you do not try to formulate rebuttals or pass any sort of judgment on what is being said. Your job is to listen to what your child or teen has to say, not judge it. Feel glad that your child chose to confide in you and make sure you do not betray that trust that was given through snarky asides or by spending so much time focusing on a response that you did not pay enough attention to the message your child was trying to convey.
4. Make it clear to your teen or child that he is more than welcome to feel any way he pleases, so long as he does not allow those feelings to spill over into his behavior in ways that are negative or unproductive. When his behaviors do become negative as well, make sure that you emphasize that the behaviors are what are being discouraged, not the emotion itself.

5. Try to relate to your child or teen when they approach you with negative feelings. Let them speak, and when they have, try to relate to them somehow. If your teen is upset about his first breakup, relate it to yours and how you felt as well. If your child is disappointed that his sandcastle fell down, tell him about a time that something you were working on did not go according to plan and how you felt. This makes them feel as though their emotions are legitimate.
6. Never tell your child or teen that she is overreacting, that she is okay, or say anything else that implies that her feelings are not accurate, justified, or acceptable. Your child or teen is free to feel however she pleases, and any feeling is legitimate.
7. After your child or teen has finished speaking, ask questions that further the conversation or that may help guide him toward a logical solution to whatever is triggering the emotions that were brought up in the first place.
8. Have an open-door policy—anything that is said to you is said in confidence unless you believe that your child or teen is breaking laws, at risk of being hurt, or someone else is at risk of being hurt. You want your child to be able to come to you with anything without fear of judgment, no matter what.
9. Never suggest to your teen, especially to daughters, that their emotions are actually just hormones and are an over-reaction. Your daughter's feelings are no less valid just because she is a girl, and implying that they are less trustworthy is sexist and unfair to her.
10. Never tell your child or teen that crying is unacceptable. Crying is a legitimate expression of emotion and is not a harmful behavior to anyone around. It should not be belittled or discouraged, as doing so will only encourage your child to hide emotions altogether, rather than encouraging an open conversation about their emotions.

10 Tips for Labeling Your Child or Teen's Emotions

1. Make it a point to name your child or teen's emotion in conversations regarding them. This not only acknowledges and validates the emotion and shows that you are paying attention, but also allows children in particular to develop a wider vocabulary involving emotions. Every time you name your child or teen's emotions, make sure you use a handful of similar, but still different words that would describe the emotion to give your child or teen some variety and options.
2. Name your own emotions when talking to your child or teen about how something that directly affected you. If your child did not put away his Legos and you stepped on one, tell him that it made you very sad and angry to step on one because it really hurt. If your teen was out past curfew and did not answer his phone, tell him how afraid you were and how much you worried until you finally got a hold of him.
3. Find a picture of a feelings wheel online and print it out. Whenever your child or teen is getting overwhelmed or upset, encourage her to go to the feelings wheel and pick out a middle or outer level word to explain her feelings to you in a word that is more specific than angry, sad, or bad.
4. Give your teen the feelings wheel that you printed out for your younger child and encourage him to use outer words as well in a conversation. Turn it into a game—whoever can use the most specific language about their emotions wins.
5. Give the entire family copies of blank bingo sheets and have each person fill it out with outer level words from the feelings wheel. Set up a movie for movie night and try to identify the emotions on your chart on characters in the movie. You must write down the context for each emotion on your chart as well for ease of remembering when it happened. The first person to bingo is the winner.

DEVELOPING EMOTIONAL INTELLIGENCE

6. Encourage your child to identify how other children at the playground are feeling and to tailor her interactions with them accordingly. This gets her thinking about what emotions look like in other people, allowing her to practice some empathy.
7. Play emotional charades with your teen or child that can read independently. This gets the entire family involved and thinking about emotions. Take all of the outer emotions from the feelings wheel and put them in a basket or some other container. Take turns picking out one slip of paper and trying to act out the emotion written on the slip without using words. Whoever guesses correctly gets to keep that slip of paper. Whoever has the most slips by the end of the game is the winner.
8. Role-play or play dolls with your child and make emotions important. Make an annoyed face or gesture, or have your doll say, "Yuck!" in a disgusted tone and ask your child to identify the emotion she thinks your doll is feeling. Encourage her to keep trying until she guesses the right one. After your child identifies the emotion you were portraying, ask her to act one out and tell her that she will win if she can come up with one you cannot identify. Go back and forth, practicing the emotional exchanges.
9. Praise your child or teen any time they come to you to discuss their emotions unprompted, and offer even more praise if they use emotionally intelligent words or seek to be specific with their emotions. For example, if your child tells you he is frustrated, or your teen tells you that he is particularly livid today, those expressions would deserve extra praise compared to your child saying he feels bad.
10. Make emotions collage with your child. Give your child a bunch of old magazines, scissors, and glue, and have them find pictures of people showing signs of various emotions to paste in clusters on their paper. Give her four or five categories of emotions to discover within the magazines. For children not yet reading, you can draw faces with the appropriate emotion to label each category.

Put the completed collage up on the fridge, and encourage your child to run to point at whatever emotion she is feeling at any given moment.

DEVELOPING EMOTIONAL INTELLIGENCE

10 Tips for Encouraging Your Child or Teen to Problem Solve

1. Ask your child or teen guiding questions when they feel stuck or otherwise unable to solve their problem. These guiding questions, such as, "what do you think would happen if I tried this?" help point the child in the right direction without necessarily giving them the right answer, especially if you make your suggestion just slightly flawed enough to not work, but close enough to the solution that they can figure it out with some more thought.
2. When your child or teen is overwhelmed, encourage him to identify the problem at hand. This problem could be something minor, such as being annoyed about not getting ice cream, or as major as struggling in class due to losing a parent. Once the problem is identified, solutions are easier to find. It is next to impossible to find the answer to questions you do not yet know.
3. Problem solving also entails making sure behaviors are not out of line. Emotionally charged behaviors can become a problem or make the problem worse. Remind children and teens that while all emotions are accepted, misbehaviors need to be managed and controlled. Reminders of consequences for adults may be appropriate, depending on consequences, such as losing a job if responsibilities are not met.
4. Remember, this is a work in progress. Do not expect your child or teen to suddenly be a master at emotional problem solving, especially if it is not something you have worked to strengthen much before now. Your child or teen will learn in time, so long as you give her the time she needs. Your patience on the topic will make this step far more bearable.
5. Do not set your child up for failure! Children thrive in environments in which they are free to explore without fear of overstepping or being told no. If you can create an environment at home in which no is a rarely spoken word, your child will develop

stronger problem-solving abilities simply due to not running into constant situations in which he is told no or has his creativity quashed for any reason at all.

6. Remember, teens are impulsive. The part of the brain that regulates impulses and weighs those impulses against risk is not yet developed and will not be until later in adulthood. Your teen may be likely to take risks that are not necessarily smart due to this. You should be prepared, especially if peer pressure gets involved. Teens may try to engage in risky behavior, which will only further get them into trouble. You should make sure they are armed with the knowledge they need prior to being in a dangerous situation.

7. Set up a code word that means your teen needs you to get them out of a risky or dangerous situation. Furthering the ideas in the previous section, setting up a safe word that your teen can text you provides your teen with an out for situations in which she may not feel comfortable or safe without her losing face to her peers. Because her peers will see her parent calling and demanding she comes home, she instantly has an excuse they will not argue with, and she is able to avoid a situation she wanted nothing to do with in the first place.

8. One of the best ways to develop problem-solving skills is to allow your child or teen to fail sometimes, especially if the situation is controlled. Allowing your child to fail and flounder a bit forces them to try to solve the problem on their own, forcing critical thinking skills, while you are still present if your child may need you. It is the best of both worlds, allowing for independence while also providing the safety net of a parent.

9. Both your teen and child should be encouraged to think up multiple solutions to any given problem. Ask her to think about the problem at hand and offer three or four solutions to it. Once those solutions have been brainstormed, ask her to weigh both the pros and cons for each solution. This then gives her a way to

compare the various solutions against each other and discover the one that will have the best results for her.
10. Last, but certainly not least, you should encourage your child or teen to remain persistent. Failure is a part of life, and it almost certainly will happen repeatedly to him. He needs to be prepared to face that fact while also being willing to keep trying after a failure has happened. The only way to go after failing is up, and even if he continues to fail, he will be no worse off than he already was. This step may require extra encouragement—failing is hard, even for people who have finished developing!

23

Recommended Children's Books to Help with Emotional Intelligence and Emotion Coaching

Books for Toddlers and Preschoolers

Story of My Feelings by Laurie Berkner: Paired with a CD with a song, popular children's music artist Laurie Berkner teaches children about their feelings and how all feelings are valid and have a purpose. Young children will love the music paired with cute illustrations and meaningful lyrics that will keep your child bouncing to the beat and fully engaged with the story. This is good for identifying basic emotions and teaching how emotions and behaviors are related.

My Mouth Is a Volcano! by Julia Cook: This book follows Louis, who always interrupts those around him. As soon as his thoughts pop into his mind, his mouth erupts, and he cannot help but tell those around him whatever has popped up with no regard to who was talking or if he was hurting someone else's feelings by interrupting them. Louis then gets interrupted, and he begins to understand the effect of interrupting people as they talk. He begins to think empathetically about the situation, and the child learns a fun technique for controlling his or her words until it is appropriate to chime in.

Dealing with Feelings Series by Elizabeth Crary: These books, aimed toward younger children, recognize the child's feelings, and guide the child through the process of dealing with them. It provides age-appropriate suggestions for coping with emotions and introduces children, and their parents, to the idea that there are better ways to deal with emotions than to react impulsively.

Books for Children

My Dragon Books Series by Steve Herman: These books explore a wide range of feelings, from grief to anxiety, coping with change, and dealing with many more negative or powerful emotions. They follow a boy and his dragon, Diggory, through the various stages of emotions, as well as what your child can do to feel better, in easily understood language formatted with rhymes. With adorable illustrations and an idea that keeps a child's attention, this is a must-have series to coping with emotions, aimed toward kindergarteners-2nd graders.

Angry Octopus by Lori Lite: This story introduces your child to an octopus who feels angry about discovering his garden destroyed one morning. The octopus works through learning to manage his anger through a series of deep breaths and relaxing muscles, one by one. This book reads more like a guided meditation for your child and encourages him or her to follow along with the angry octopus and learn to relax on cue. It helps children understand the idea of anger, as well as emotional triggers while providing a coping mechanism for that anger to avoid lashing out unnecessarily, even in the face of anger that can feel almost overwhelming.

Alexander and the Terrible, Horrible, No Good, Very Bad Day by Judith Viorst: This book is a children's classic for a reason. Your child will follow Alexander as he has a day that just gets worse and worse. The ending offers little in terms of problem-solving or offering hope for the next day to be better, with the moral of the story being that sometimes, people just have bad days, and that is okay. This book is a fantastic stepping stone into conversations about Alexander's emotions, as well as how he could have behaved differently to see different results.

Books for Tweens and Teens

Conquer Negative Thinking for Teens by Mary Karapetian Alvord and Anne McGrath: This book, aimed toward teens, helps teach them to identify patterns of negative thinking that could be negatively impacting their emotions, and therefore their behavior. Being able to control those negative thoughts is a crucial skill to mastering the self-management side of emotional intelligence, and this book will help teens focus on various types of negative thoughts while also teaching them the skills necessary to overcome those emotions. With easily understood language with an appropriate pace, assignments, and activities that are easily executed, and plenty of advice, this book will help motivated teens to manage their emotions and behaviors.

The Feelings Book: The Care & Keeping of Your Emotions by Dr. Lynda Madison: While this book may skew toward the tween end of this spectrum, there is valuable information that teens could learn hidden within these pages. A companion to the ever-popular *The Care & Keeping of You*, this book is primarily aimed toward girls, though the information within it could largely be applied toward boys.

Don't Let Your Emotions Run Your Life for Teens by Sheri Van Dijk: This book is a workbook aimed to teach your teen how to manage mood swings, anger, and other strong emotions. This book approaches emotions from a dialectical behavior therapy standpoint and guides your teen through the steps of becoming aware of thoughts and how to cope with them, along with plenty of examples included within.

24

Conclusion

Congratulations! You have finished *Emotional Intelligence for Kids*! If you have made it this far, you likely have a pretty good idea of your strengths and weaknesses regarding your parenting style. You may be parenting in a style that you wish was different, or you may realize that your own EQ is not high enough for you to effectively emotion coach your child through their own emotions. No matter where you stand, hopefully, the information you found within these pages provided you with insight for where to go from here to better your own emotion coaching skills.

Regardless of whether your next step is to begin working on your own emotional intelligence or jumping right into emotion coaching your child, you should have found valuable information to help you on your journey. If you are planning to focus on yourself first to get your own EQ to a level that would be conducive to emotion coaching, try checking out Emotional Intelligence 2.0 and Emotional Intelligence Practical Guide. These two parts will provide complementary information to what was found in this one and will give you the guidance and skills you need to prepare to raise an emotionally intelligent child.

If you are ready to move on to emotion coaching your child, remember the key steps to emotion coaching: being aware of your child's emotions, seeing emotions as learning opportunities for your child, listening to and validating your child's feelings, labeling emotions, and helping your child to problem-solve. Each of these steps will help your child build up the foundations of emotional intelligence that will carry your child through life and help your child develop the skills to flourish socially.

Remember to avoid over- or under-correcting your own behaviors and parenting styles and creating unintended effects with your child. Remember, moderation is important in all things, and too much of any good thing can have unintended consequences. Overcorrecting can be just as bad as under-correcting, especially if you swing from too permissive to too controlling.

As you take your first steps in your emotion coaching journey, remember to keep in mind the most important part of the process: Being an involved, empathetic, and supporting parent. This will help strengthen your bond with your child, encouraging your relationship with him or her, and you may even find your relationship evolving into something better than you ever could have imagined as your child learns how to better communicate and regulate feelings. The end result will be a happier child, a happier parent, and less conflict overall. With less conflict and misunderstandings, both you and your child will be able to truly enjoy spending time together without worrying about meltdowns or arguments. Lastly, remember to keep moving forward, even if you run into hardships from time to time. There will be struggles and roadblocks, but you will get past them, and your child will learn from watching you persevere in the face of adversity.

www.ingramcontent.com/pod-product-compliance
Lightning Source LLC
Chambersburg PA
CBHW071609080526
44588CB00010B/1078